HAUNTED BAY CITY MICHIGAN

NICOLE BEAUCHAMP

Haunted America

Published by Haunted America
A Division of The History Press
Charleston, SC
www.historypress.com

Front cover image copyright of Amy Shabluk.
Back cover images copyright of Bill Randall.

First published 2020

Manufactured in the United States

ISBN 9781467146708

Library of Congress Control Number: 2020938679

Notice: The information in this book is true and complete to the best of our knowledge. It is offered without guarantee on the part of the author or The History Press. The author and The History Press disclaim all liability in connection with the use of this book.

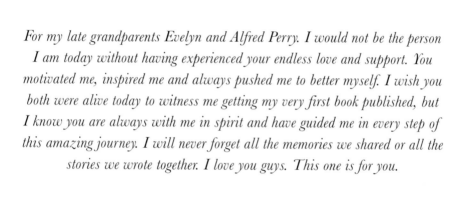

For my late grandparents Evelyn and Alfred Perry. I would not be the person I am today without having experienced your endless love and support. You motivated me, inspired me and always pushed me to better myself. I wish you both were alive today to witness me getting my very first book published, but I know you are always with me in spirit and have guided me in every step of this amazing journey. I will never forget all the memories we shared or all the stories we wrote together. I love you guys. This one is for you.

CONTENTS

ACKNOWLEDGEMENTS

Writing a book has been a dream of mine since I was a little girl. There have been a lot of people who have helped to make this dream a reality for me. First, I want to thank John Rodrigue from The History Press for presenting me with this opportunity and having enough faith in me to undertake a project like this. This would never have been a possibility if not for you. To my mother, Ellen; father, Harold; brother, Bruce; Aunt Amy, Aunt Irina, Uncle Rex and Uncle Mike; and cousins Perry, Lauren, Alex, Sasha and Maria. Thank you for loving me and supporting me in all my endeavors (and I know there have been many). You guys mean the world to me, and I love all of you so much! To Stephanie Gatza for always believing in me even when I did not believe in myself. You had my back when I needed a push. I could not have done this without you. To Frances Kermeen for being an inspiration to me and for encouraging me to write my own book. To Kati Jones and Carrie and Reanna Crowl for being awesome friends and being there when I needed you most. To Bobby Jereb for always going out of your way for me in order to make this project the best that it could be. To Bill Randall (Saginaw Valley Naval Ship Museum) for spending an entire day with me and trekking through marshes to get good back cover material for the book. You both have been a huge part of this project and helped me so much with the entire photo process. Your efforts are greatly appreciated, and you both should be proud, because this is your success as well. I am truly so honored to call such amazing people my lifelong friends.

To Kristen Sanborn for sharing your beautiful photos of the Scottish Rite Masonic Center with me. To the owners, staff and volunteers of the locations I wrote about: Michael Kegley, Carla Monteiro and Bill Randall (of course!) from the Saginaw Valley Naval Ship Museum; Chris Sova and Nancy Williams from the Scottish Rite Masonic Center; Elaine Fournier from the Bay City Antiques Center; Kirsten Grantham-Wellnitz from Sage Public Library; Nick Suchyta, Kelley Kent and Adam Gac from the Friends of the Historic Masonic Temple; Starr and Michael Henning from Tummy Ache Candy Store; James Forest Goodrow, Lisa Goodrow and Jenae Prell from Bayshire Beauty Academy; Heidi Prince and Pastor Jon Essex from the former Memorial Presbyterian Church; Shannon and Justin Rodriguez from Voodoo Tattoo and the former Belle Epoque Art Gallerie; Brenda Baker and Paul Phillips from the State Theatre; Brennan Benedict from Old City Hall Restaurant; and everyone else who assisted me with this project. Your time and efforts in meeting and corresponding with me on your days off, proofreading my chapters, photo donations and generally just being super supportive of my work has left a lasting positive effect on me. Thank you for trusting me to tell your stories.

A big thank-you to the paranormal community, which has accepted me as a fellow weirdo from day one. I have found my happy place in life, and it is among all of you. A special thank-you to Tim Shaw, Johna Shorey, Hunter Roebuck, the Smith Sisters, Ashley Harris and Adam Wcislek (Spirit World Paranormal Investigations, SWPI) for being so generous in contributing your personal experiences to my book. It is not always easy to share one's personal experiences with the world, and your bravery is admirable.

To the various historical societies, archive collectors, historians and libraries that helped me find tons of records, news articles, books and historic photographs and resources, such as Mary Ruthko from the Bay County Library System, Mark Grotelueschen of the Alice and Jack Wirt Public Library, Jeanette Marks from the Pinconning Branch Library, Mark Peter Sprang from the Historical Collections of the Great Lakes at Bowling Green University, Peter Corina and Laura Linke from Cornell University, Kathleen Weessies from Michigan State University, historian Priscilla Massie, Jared Yax from the Tri-Cities Historical Museum, Samantha Mayo from the Historical Division of the USMC Archives, Janet O'Keefe from the Flint Public Library, Jim Gerencser from the Carlisle Indian School, Jonathan Roscoe from the Naval History and Heritage Command, Ron Bloomfield of Central Michigan University and every other person and organization that extended a helping hand to me—and believe me, there were many—thank you from the bottom of my heart! Even though I could not use all the materials that were sent to me or that I had requested, I would not have had such a plethora of options if not for you! I want to say thank you to the rest of the staff at the Bay County Library System for not only helping me with research but also allowing me to host annual lectures at your libraries and promoting my events with so much enthusiasm.

I want to give a special shout-out to Jane Anderson for taking a chance on me in the very beginning, when I requested to do my very first "big" lecture at the Alice and Jack Wirt Public Library. I owe so much of my success to you. Thank you to Heather Radina of Beauty Within salon for making me look amazing in my headshot and thank you to the incredible Laurie Kuligoski for the beautiful portrait you took of me. A giant thank-you to Amy Shabluk from Portraits by Amy Michelle for producing the most perfect front cover photo ever! I appreciate you for being so adaptive to the crazy demands that were put on you. I want to acknowledge the rest of my friends, extended family, social media followers and paranormal team for always having faith in me and giving me a reason to wake up every day. Your love is what motivates me to never give up. Last, but not least, thank you to everyone who decided to give this book a chance and purchase it. I have so much love for you! Thanks for being a part of the journey!

PREFACE

Haunted. The term itself evokes many emotions within people. It can stir up pure terror in some, while others find it fascinating. As someone who founded the Tri-City Ghost Hunters Society, a paranormal research team, in 2009, it is safe to say I have been in a myriad of purportedly haunted locations. I have traveled the country and the world seeking the truth about what happens when we die. Due to all my years of research and experiences within the field, my perception of the word *haunted* is different than most individuals. To me, the term *haunted* is not always synonymous with *demonic* or *negative*. I can only blame horror movies and TV shows for treating every paranormal case like a dealing with the devil. Just as with people, there is diversity in the paranormal realm. Sure, there have been some scary things we've had to deal with in years of doing this kind of work, but most of the time, it's just people like you and me who aren't ready to leave this Earth yet.

Of course, it is understandable how unsettling this type of activity can be to those who are not used to it and have not been previously exposed to it. I did not get into the paranormal because of a television show or because it was the popular thing to do. In fact, I had a lifelong interest in ghosts, and once I had my own experiences with the paranormal as a small child, I wanted to discover more about them and the inspiring idea of life after death.

Every year, I am invited to lecture at libraries and universities across the state to share my paranormal evidence and educate the public on what it

Tri-City Ghost Hunters Society. *Courtesy of MLive Media Group, 2019, used with permission.*

is like to be a researcher. I adore these opportunities to speak with others and enlighten the community on what it is that I do, because I am also able to promote my love for history and stress the importance of historical preservation. As I always say, the paranormal and history go hand in hand. Since I have started my team, we have supported and given thousands of dollars to historical preservation efforts across the globe. Some buildings that were in utter despair have been fully renovated to their former grandeur with our continual hard work. That being said, our team is only one of many teams out there that deeply cares about history and the lifespan of these antiqued structures.

The media has a special way of portraying teams of our kind as a careless, heartless bunch. "Ghost Hunters Burn Down Historic Mansion"—we have all read a headline like that at one time or another. But I am here to tell you that those people are not true ghost hunters; they are heartless criminals with zero respect for the beauty of the past. Ghost hunters, paranormal investigators, spirit seekers—in my opinion are all one in the same—whatever term people choose to identify with is up to them, but we are a good community of people and we fight every day to distance ourselves from the villain-like persona that society likes to pin on us.

I've hand-selected the locales in this book, as they are places that I am passionate about, and some of them were even personally investigated by my team. The various stories within the text contain historical discoveries of those whose souls have not yet crossed over. I have worked closely with each location's owners, volunteers, staff, patrons and visitors to represent the city's haunted in the most respectful of ways. These individuals deserve to have their stories told and be validated. Throughout this book, I am able to take each reader on heartwarming and bone-chilling journeys of the past and present in my hometown of Bay City. I hope you enjoy the ride. Next stop, Hell's Half Mile.

Introduction

The Summer City with a Haunting History

Pure Michigan. A state that is known for its picturesque landscapes and sparkling Great Lakes. When you think of Michigan, you think of Mackinaw Island, a relaxing and secluded vacation paradise. You think of the intense winters, with glittering snowflakes falling from the sky and blankets of stark-white snow covering the ground. You think of some of the best sweets money can possibly buy—thick slabs of mouthwatering fudge with endless caramel ribbons. Michigan is one of the most beautiful states to travel to within our nation. But there is more to Michigan than meets the eye. Michigan has a dark side.

At the base of the Saginaw Bay on Lake Huron lies the gorgeous historic waterfront city of Bay City, Michigan. What many people do not know is that it was originally named Lower Saginaw, as it geographically fell within Saginaw County until Bay County was established in 1857. It was at this time that the name was changed to Bay City. The earliest pioneers of Saginaw County made their way to what was then Lower Saginaw, as the shallow waters of the Saginaw settlement were not easily navigable. The newly discovered deeper waters were perfect for the growth of the lumbering industry, which relied heavily on shipping. In 1865, twenty-eight years after it was first established, Bay City was incorporated as its own city and became a bustling community of its own. The city, which is divided into the East Side and West Side by way of the Saginaw River, was at one time considered two separate cities. In 1905, the two cities became unified, and Bay City grew in size and population.

View of commercial buildings on Center Avenue in Bay City, Michigan. Printed on front: "Center Avenue, looking east, Bay City, Mich." Printed on back: "4562. Pub. by I. Korn 'The Washington' Bay City, Mich." *Courtesy of the Burton Historical Collection, Detroit Public Library.*

In the summer months, the city is booming with tourism. Individuals travel far and wide to witness the majestic fireworks display in celebration of Independence Day (one of the largest in the entire country) and to stroll the riverfront during the Tall Ships Celebration to view vintage sailing ships from all over the world. Both events border closely the eighteen blocks of East Bay City's downtown historic district. If these streets could talk, what would they say? Perhaps they would tell the tales of how vastly different downtown is today in comparison to the past.

Originally a camping ground for Native Americans of the Chippewa tribe, Bay City soon became a mecca for fur traders and lumberjacks alike. From 1865 to 1900, rowdy saloons, gambling houses, sordid hotels and brothels all made up a six-block strip known as Hell's Half Mile that occupied the Third Street Bridge area. That's right, Bay City had a red-light district, and it was a terribly dangerous place to be, with an abundance of violence and debauchery. In fact, every spring, when the lumbermen arrived in the city, the locals—apart from the city's seedy characters—would avoid going downtown at all costs. After all, the prostitutes in the district were thought to be the most beautiful in the region, and they were plentiful. Cassie Hawkins, who had earned her reputation as the most upscale entertainer, operated the most expensive bordello in the city, charging men five dollars for a service. Men believed she had a likeness to Lillian Russell, one of the most famous actresses and singers of that period.

At this time, the local economy was largely influenced by lumber processing, and Bay City earned its reputation as the "Lumbering Capital of the World." Due to the hearty size of the trees in the area, by 1882, there was a whopping 112 sawmills lining the Saginaw River. Anywhere from five to ten thousand lumbermen would make their way from northern Michigan to Bay City to celebrate the end of lumbering season with their hard-earned money, which was only about $150. Surely, in today's money, $150 would not go far, but at this time, you could stay at a hotel for only $1 per day or hire a lady of the night for a mere $0.50. The corner of Third and Water Streets was the hub of self-indulgence for these men. A series of underground tunnels and catacombs allowed them to access the thirty-seven saloons and eighty houses of ill repute without ever being seen. This system helped the shanty boys, as the lumbermen were called back then, avoid encounters with law enforcement officials. Brawling, boozing, swindling, murder and other various forms of corruption were all-day, everyday occurrences during this time. After all, a typical logging season consisted of

An old postcard of the Third Street Bridge. *Courtesy of Mark Peter Sprang of the Institute for Great Lakes Research, Bowling Green State University.*

Log boom retaining logs on Saginaw Bay. Four men, somewhat formally dressed, sitting on boom. Freighter in the distance. Printed on mat front: "Photographed by G.F. Sterling, West Bay City, Mich." June 19, 1889. *Courtesy of the Burton Historical Collection, Detroit Public Library.*

spending up to six months outside with soaking wet socks and boots while performing one of the most laborious jobs in history, all for a measly $20 to $45 a month. That would be enough to drive anyone crazy.

Fabian Fournier, better known as "Joe Fournier" or "Saginaw Joe," was crazy alright. He was a legendary French Canadian lumberman who raised hell anywhere that he went. In comparison to the other lumberjacks, Joe, who was considered a big and burly man of the era, stood about six feet in height. While his strength and tall stature allowed him to demonstrate proficiency at his job, he was feared by those around him due to his large size and aggressive nature. He had combative tendencies and a relentless thirst for blood. After the Civil War ended, the Quebec native made his way to Michigan in order to take advantage of the profitable opportunities in the lumbering industry. However, no amount of money in the world could have prevented Fournier from wanting to brawl. He was constantly looking for a fight. In 1875, Fournier finally met his end, as he was killed during an altercation at the ferry boat dock on Water Street. He left behind a wife and two children—although they likely did not see much of him anyhow.

He was anything but a loyal family man. His notoriety lives on through the American folklore story of Paul Bunyan.

One lumberman who rivaled Joe Fournier as being the most outrageous in the history of Bay City was Thomas C. Cunnion, also known as T.C. Cunnion. Thomas, born and raised in Peterborough, Ontario, referred to himself as the "Man-Eater." He traumatized the citizens of Saginaw by gnawing on a piece of bloody cow liver as if he were a lion with a fresh kill. He later made his way to Bay City, where he continued to scar people with his offensive and off-the-wall antics. He would physically fight bulldogs in dens on Water Street for free alcoholic drinks. He would become dog-like during the battles by growling and biting as if he was a wild animal. I am sure we could all agree that Bay City's entertainment has drastically improved since then.

It is no doubt that today, our world has witnessed true atrocities at the hands of humans, but this kind of turbulence was commonplace in Bay City during the lumbering era. Seeing bodies of murder victims floating down the Saginaw River was as normal as seeing a boat out there today. The St. James Saloon, which sat where Wenona Park is today, was one of many places to go for a person seeking trouble. Near the saloon, a strange individual called "Happy Jack Ryan" hid underneath a women's outhouse hoping to catch a peek of female flesh, only to get arrested instead. Another man known only as "Carpenter" brutally scalped a man, while Owen McGivern bit off Frank Teuro's nose after a drunken brawl at the Third Street Saloon. In these days, having your nose bitten off was as natural as throwing a punch, especially among drunks. "Brick" Thomas, one of Bay City's most notorious characters, was arrested nearly three hundred times. Anyone who found themselves in a quarrel with a feisty lumberman were subject to what was labelled "logger's smallpox," the inevitable disfigurement one would endure after being kicked in the face by a pair of spiky boots. To top it all off, a transplant from Toronto named Emmaline, known historically as "Canada Em," was one of Bay City's prostitutes. She goes down in history as the only person in the city to actually be buried alive. She was thrown into a detention cell in the basement of the Old City Hall restaurant, which used to be the city's jail. The police station occupied the bar, while the courthouse inhabited the restaurant portion.

Visitors to the basement can still see the two solitary confinement cells that were left behind when the jail was torn down—only they are now being used as storage units for the eatery. Emmaline's death was credited to insanity, and she was promptly buried first thing in the morning. What

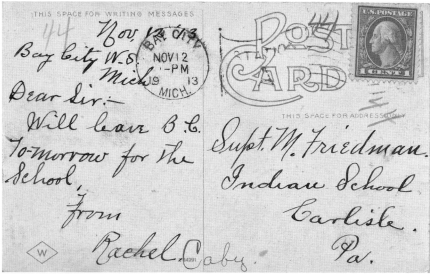

A postcard showcasing a river scene from Wenonah Park, Bay City. *Courtesy of Jim Gerencser, Carlisle Indian School, Digital Resource Center.*

they didn't know was that she was having a catatonic fit, which perfectly explained her unresponsive stupor. Her boyfriend Bay City Bart dug up her body after suspicions that law enforcement had sent her corpse to the University of Michigan's medical school, but it was apparent upon opening the casket that she had been buried prematurely. Based on the

A solitary-confinement cell in the basement of Old City Hall Restaurant in Bay City. *Courtesy of Brennan Benedict.*

positioning of her body and her hair in complete disarray, there was no doubt that she had been fighting hard for her life. The most chilling aspect? The claw marks that marred the wood inside the coffin. While Emmaline's story remains one of a kind, there are so many stories of destruction, devastation and pure brutality that could make one very thankful for not being around during that particular time in history. Nowadays, if you decide to dine in at the Old City Hall, look for the woman in an elegant red ball gown. That is just Emmaline going about her unfinished business.

While the amoral side of Hell's Half Mile was being eradicated at the turn of the century by way of a stronger police force and has since been replaced with charming coffee shops, cute boutiques and other well-received establishments, the proof of this deviant time in history is literally right under our feet. That is because the underground tunnels and catacombs of the city still exist. Sure, they are not as easily accessible as they once were, but they hold some of the deepest, darkest secrets in the entire history of Bay City. Keep in mind, however, that Hell's Half Mile is only one of many histories. Each building, each home, each district and each possession in Bay City and in every other place across the globe all have their own individual stories. The telling of these tales is imperative in order to keep history alive.

1
THE GRAY GHOST

When crossing the Independence Bridge, you cannot help but be captivated by the impressive blue-gray ship that has found its home on the Saginaw River. Year after year, people come to the USS *Edson* (DD-946) for a multitude of reasons—to honor its arduous journey across the world, to pay respects to current and retired military personnel, to learn about how sailors worked at sea, to participate in special community events and even to partake in paranormal investigations with the hopes of contacting seamen from beyond the grave. However, this Forrest Sherman–class destroyer almost didn't make it to Bay City. The former Defoe Shipyard, which used to build ships just like the *Edson*, was intended to be the home of the USS *Charles F. Adams*. Upon inspection, it was discovered that the USS *Charles F. Adams* was in such poor condition that it would cost upward of $1 million to renovate it to a museum-grade attraction. Between the ship being in such poor shape and political disagreements on its intended use, it was eventually sold to a scrap company in 2020. The *Edson*, being in substantially better physical condition, was much more cost effective at $750,000 to purchase and transport from the Philadelphia Naval Shipyard to Bay City via the St. Lawrence Seaway on May 7, 2013.

The USS *Edson*'s legacy was born on December 3, 1956, in Bath, Maine, at the Bath Iron Works Shipyard. Due to the tradition of naming naval destroyers after American naval leaders and heroes, the ship became a symbol of honor for Major General Merritt Austin Edson, a U.S. marine who was awarded the Medal of Honor for his services in the Pacific theater.

Official portrait, Major General M. Edson, USMC (Ret'd). Hdqtrs. No. A-48479. DEFENSE DEPT. PHOTO (Marine Corps). Staff Sergeant Gordon W. Matheson. *Courtesy of Samantha Mayo, USMC Archives, History Division.*

On January 4, 1958, the *Edson*'s official launching ceremony was hosted by Ethel Robbins Edson, General Edson's widow. The *Edson* eventually arrived at its home port of Long Beach, California, after sailing through the Caribbean, Panama Canal and Lima, Peru. For the next twenty years, the *Edson* served in the Pacific Fleet, where it earned the nickname "The Destroyer" and was recognized as a "Top Gun" ship. Five of its Western Pacific deployments led it into the Vietnamese war zone. One incident took place off the coast of Vietnam in 1968, when *Edson* was struck by enemy gunfire. It was reported to enemy troops that it was sunk with no survivors due to the attack. What the enemy troops did not know, however, was that *Edson* had sailed into the Subic Bay of the Philippines and was promptly repaired. Once *Edson* was in working order again, it reappeared off the coast of Vietnam. The enemy troops stood in shock at the sight and believed that they were seeing a phantom ship. It was at this point the destroyer was nicknamed "The Gray Ghost," a title it holds to this day. The *Edson*'s last decade of service included sailing to its new homeport of Newport, Rhode Island. It was eventually decommissioned by Commander Gideon W. Almy III, USN, on December 15, 1988, and later transported to New York City to serve as a portion of the Intrepid Sea-Air-Space Museum for a multitude of years. The U.S. Navy reacquired the ship with the intention to scrap it. The Saginaw Valley Naval Ship Museum's president, Michael Kegley, who had served twenty-eight years in the navy as a chief petty officer, refused to allow that to happen. After all, this ship had survived harrowing battles at sea and lived on as a monument of American strength and perseverance. Not only that, but it is only one of two surviving Forrest Sherman–class destroyers present in the world today.

The director of the New York City Intrepid Museum, Gary Spampanato, had a son named Paul who was the ship's primary caretaker and manager for over a decade. He had many duties aboard the ship, including painting,

USS *Edson* (DD-946) undergoes repair in AFDM-5 in Subic Bay, Republic of the Philippines, June 1967. *Official U.S. Navy photo by R.D. Moeser, JOC, courtesy of National Archives, catalog no. USN 1142189.*

chipping rust off the decks and offering below-deck tours. What started out as a simple volunteering gig for Paul turned into his full-blown passion over time. Paul, who had worked on aircrafts in the service, originally joined the Intrepid Museum as the director of ships force. With this title, he managed tour guide staff and maintenance of both the USS *Edson* and a submarine by the name of *Growler*. Over time, Paul became so infatuated and meticulous with the *Edson* that it became the sole focus of his volunteer efforts. His entire life became dedicated to ensuring that the ship was in immaculate condition. While aboard the *Edson*, he always wore his khaki uniform of a chief petty officer. His father, Gary, recalled Paul being so fascinated with the ship that it was his only focal point: "There was only one subject for him, the USS *Edson*." Paul even informed his father that being on the *Edson* made him so happy, he preferred to die aboard. Eerily, on Thanksgiving Day, November 25, 1999, Paul met his fate after having a heart attack aboard the warship. The only other death reported on the *Edson* was during its days in combat when a sailor was crushed by a falling box in the cargo hold. A year after Paul's death, a ceremony was held on the *Edson* in which he was posthumously recognized with the Casper J. Knight Jr. Award from the Historic Naval Ships Association, which acknowledged his hard work and dedication to the Gray Ghost.

Bill Randall, a six-year navy veteran, recalls walking through the Bay City Mall one day and stumbling upon Michael Kegley dressed in his officer uniform and holding a donation jar to raise money for the ship. Having worked aboard a naval destroyer as a machine repairman and second-class petty officer during his time in the service, Bill felt inspired to volunteer at the *Edson*. Kegley informed Bill that he was looking for tour guides, and Bill excitedly jumped at the opportunity to help out. He began his volunteer position with the Saginaw Valley Naval Ship Museum in 2013. Bill recalled an unsettling experience while he was down in what is referred to as the 9/11 Room, a room that was used to aid emergency responders during the September 11, 2001 terrorist attacks. Two sailors came to visit the ship, and Bill took them on a private tour in some areas of the ship that the general public isn't allowed. After the sailors left for the evening, Bill began closing up shop. As he walked through the ship, he flicked off the light switches to each room as he exited. He started at the port side door of forward berthing from the 9/11 Room and came up to the starboard side door. Upon exiting, he had realized that the port side door was closed and sealed shut. "Metal on metal doors make a lot of noise, and I never heard anything. At the time, I was only about twenty feet away. If someone was there, I should have and would have heard them." That was his first incident. As a former skeptic, he called down to the office and asked who was just on the ship to make sure he was not locking anyone in and was told that he was alone.

During a sweltering Saturday night in mid-August, a public ghost hunt was hosted that Bill Randall participated in. Some of the guests asked him about the farthest access point on the ship below decks. As someone very familiar with this particular style of ship, he led the paranormal investigators in complete darkness to the boatswain's locker. This portion of the ship was utilized by boatswain's mates (individuals who were responsible for caring for the outside of the ship) as a closet for storing paint, grease, tools and so forth. Seven investigators were present that night, including Bill. At the time, there was no electrical power in the forward portion of the ship, so the group navigated by flashlight. One of the ladies in the group, a paranormal investigator visiting from England, felt the temperature in the locker begin to drop, despite it being so hot and humid on the ship. Another investigator

Right: Bill Randall in the 9/11 Room, where he had his first paranormal encounter. *Courtesy of Bill Randall.*

Below: "Release Date: May 5, 1967—The USS *Edson* (DD-946) breaks away after refueling from USS *Bon Homme* Richard (CVA-31) in the South China Sea off the coast of Vietnam." *Official U.S. Navy photo by R.D. Moeser, JOC, courtesy of National Archives, catalog. no L45-83.01.04.*

suggested that her team members turn on a paranormal investigation device called a spirit box, which channels spirit voices via radio frequency. After the team turned on the spirit box, the room became colder and colder, until the English lady was shivering. She cautiously asked, "Is anyone here with us?" and a faint voice responded, "Yes." "Thanks for your response," the English lady chimed in, "but could you please tell us your name?" A distinctly male voice came through on the box and said, "My name is Paul." "Paul, when did you pass away?" The same male voice responded with a muffled number ending in nine. It was at this time that one of the young women with the group was up on the second level of the boatswain's locker and felt an arm around her waist holding her tightly so she didn't fall through the opening in the floor. She kept this a secret and afterward revealed her experience to the group. She remembers feeling that this spirit was protective of her and concerned for her safety.

The next morning, Bill came in to volunteer and decided to share his experiences with some of the other volunteers working that day. They collectively decided to search Google for real answers on who Paul was. It was at that point that they discovered the story of the late Paul Spampanato who lived aboard the *Edson* as a caretaker and tour guide. They discovered an article that was published in 2012 by the *Bay City Times* that detailed Paul's story. In shock, they called the Intrepid museum and spoke to Paul's former coworkers, gathering every detail they possibly could.

If you visit the *Edson*, do not be surprised if you spot a man wearing a khaki uniform wandering about the ship—that is just Paul making sure his precious ship is still in tip-top shape. Sightings of Paul are mostly witnessed in the wardroom, forward berthing and the ship's many winding passageways. One day, both President Michael Kegley and volunteer Jack Pennell were watching a surveillance camera that was aimed at the forward main deck on the port side of the ship and saw a man in khakis walking away from the camera. This person looked identical to the photo of Paul that was printed in the *Bay City Times* article. They surprisingly revealed that as he walked away, his body disappeared into thin air. The incident alarmed the duo, and ever since that day, Paul's presence continues to grow stronger. Visitors throughout the years have captured photos of Paul strolling the decks even when the ship was closed with no access point for the public. These experiences have made Bill Randall a believer in the afterlife. Bill believes Paul tends to be a bit of a prankster, as many visitors claim they have been tapped on the shoulder, had their hair pulled and lost possessions, despite knowing exactly where they left them. Another volunteer named Charlene was squatting down while painting a lower portion of the ship when suddenly, she was spanked by an invisible force. In a state of surprise, she whisked around to find that no one was there—at least, no one that was living.

Tim Shaw, a well-known psychic medium and lecturer, had his own experience with an entity presumed to be Paul when he was invited to the *Edson* for a paranormal event. Prior to the investigation, Tim, along with the event's attendees, was given a tour of the area aboard the ship where paranormal activity was most common. After several hours had passed of experimenting with several different spirit communication devices, the group decided to take a break. Everyone decided to head to the 9/11 Room to either rest or began reviewing any evidence. As Tim was resting, he began to feel as if eyes were on him. Never one to turn down a potential paranormal encounter, he slowly turned around and saw the darkened form of a man's body, complete with a featureless white head that resembled an over-pixelated digital image in the hatchway directly behind him. "It smoothly began to turn away from us as if it were moving on ball bearings," he said.

Tim immediately jumped up and ran after it, surprising the attendees around him.

> *I cleared the hatchway with a single hop but landed on my weak leg and bounced back and forth along the walls as I was hurrying. I saw the same figure, moving in the same fashion, turning to the left. I made it to the intersection and found nothing. There was a stairway to the upper deck, and if it had taken that route, I would have surely saw something of the phantom's exit. However, just beyond the stairway was an unlit crew berth, which I immediately entered. Scanning the darkened space with my flashlight, I checked under bunks and any furniture that would hide something of that size from my view. Nothing was found.*

When Tim returned to the group, he informed everyone of what he had seen. No one knew what to make of the experience until he spoke to Bill Randall, who told Tim that he also felt as if someone was watching him in that area. Paul was discovered deceased in the same area where Tim spotted the figure. Tim recalled, "This was one of the few peak personal experiences that I will remember for a very long time." In addition to Paul, volunteers have also encountered a ghost dog.

Bill Randall and Michael Kegley have both encountered a canine spirit. They state that they can hear a dog barking directly next to them but that they have never been able to see the dog. Bill remembered one incident when he stepped through the door on the bridge and had a ferocious-sounding dog snarl at him. It remains a mystery if Paul had a pet dog that accompanied him aboard the *Edson*. Visitors have frequently asked volunteers if there is a dog on board only to discover that there is not.

Since the *Edson* has been featured on episodes of both the *Twilight Zone* and *Ghost Asylum*, it has drawn psychics and paranormal enthusiasts to the ship from across the country and the world. Half a dozen mediums who have visited the ship have attested that eight spirits are aboard, including Paul. Adam Wcislek, known as the Black Swamp Medium and member of Spirit World Paranormal Investigations (SWPI), regularly investigates the ship and has had many strange encounters over the years.

While he has claimed to pick up on Paul's spirit, he has also picked up on other seafarers who are still reporting for duty. When initially going into these historic locations with such rich backstories, Adam prefers not to be present during a tour so that it does not influence his readings. One of his team members from SWPI decided to join him on his first visit to the ship and joined the history tour so that he could verify if Adam's readings held any merit. This man was extremely skeptical of Adam's proclaimed abilities and wanted to find out for himself if Adam could really detect the dead.

The view of the USS *Edson* from the Independence Bridge. *Courtesy of Bill Randall.*

Once the tour had concluded, Adam and his mate headed down to the engine and fire rooms deep within the bowels of the ship. Adam noted that the first step in his process is to get a feel for the energy within the location and find out if it is positive or negative. While below decks, Adam felt the presence of a sailor who was employed in the fire room. Adam remembered turning to his friend to describe the spirit in detail: "He was young, around eighteen or nineteen years old, with blond hair and blue eyes. He was drafted into the military but chose the navy because he did not want to be a foot solider. He felt things would be a lot easier." Adam continued to describe the phantom sailor's favorite thing to do once his tasks were completed. "He enjoyed swinging and building his strength through chin ups on an overhead pipe. I had very strong images of this man. Ones you just don't forget." Adam and his buddy wandered apart from each other in search of a pipe that was suitable for an individual to exercise from. Adam was drawn to an area on the ship where he had spotted an overhead bar. He recalled it being bent and, on closer inspection, had observed that the bend was indeed man-made. His friend was inspired by the incident.

The USCGC *Escanaba* being launched from the Defoe Shipyard in Bay City on September 17, 1932. This site is where the USS *Edson* is currently docked. *Courtesy of Jared Yax, Tri-Cities Historical Museum.*

Later that evening, Adam and his mate were walking among the bunks on deck when he was stopped in his tracks due to a barrage of sailors shouting their last names. He recalled it being an overwhelming experience, with some of them difficult to make out as he revealed that there were so many of them shouting. Adam began repeating the surnames aloud so that his teammate would also be a part of the experience. They continued with their stroll, and Adam's teammate let out a startling scream. "What is it?!" Adam exclaimed. With the color drained from his face, his teammate proceeded to shine his flashlight on a name tag adhered to one of the bunks. Sure enough, it was a sailor's last name that Adam had heard and voiced aloud. The encounter made Adam's skeptical friend a true believer in mediumship. Turning people into believers seems to be an ongoing trend with the *Edson*.

Perhaps on your next visit to this floating museum you will encounter something otherworldly. Maybe you will get to meet one of the many men who fought for our freedom or get to personally thank Paul for dedicating his entire existence to preserving such a valuable piece of our American history. After all, if the *Edson* had not remained in such pristine condition, it may have met the same fate as many of its fellow ships. Most importantly, do not forget to thank the countless volunteers and navy veterans who make up the Saginaw Valley Naval Ship Museum organization. Without Bay City's Gray Ghost, this town surely would not be the same.

2
FOR SALE, BUYER BEWARE

There is a belief in the paranormal community that the deceased can attach themselves to objects, particularly items that they had a strong affinity for in life. Most of us get a token of remembrance when a loved one passes on. A parent's wedding ring, a child's stuffed animal, a painting of a dear friend whose life ended too soon. For the majority of people, these objects are greatly cherished, while others believe these items create a paranormal storm within their lives. Usually, they turn them over to haunted artifact collectors, who keep these items stored away from the public, sometimes in blessed and locked containers. The most famous haunted collectors in the world were the late Ed and Lorraine Warren, who ran an occult museum from the back of their home in Monroe, Connecticut.

The most notable and notorious case in their history was when they acquired the famous Annabelle doll—a Raggedy Ann doll believed to be possessed by a demon. The doll was purchased in 1970 at an antique store by a mother who was looking for a sweet birthday gift for her daughter. After an abundance of disturbing and creepy experiences involving the doll, a paranormal investigation and an exorcism, the doll was turned over to the Warrens for storage. The Warrens have since passed away, but the doll remains locked inside a specialized wood and glass cabinet that had been soaked in holy water and holy oil. In addition to the infused case, a postcard-sized white sign bears the words "Positively, do not open," along with three crosses and two figures of St. Michael, the protector. Of course, not every haunted object holds as horrific a story as the Annabelle doll.

The theory is that spirits attach themselves to these items in order to stay connected to the dimension of the living.

If there was any chance of encountering one of these objects with an attachment, you would not have to look any further than the Bay City Antiques Center, located in the heart of what was formerly Hell's Half Mile. If you pay attention to the right of the large Antiques sign posted on the front of the building, you will see faded white letters indicative of the building's colorful past. The building at 1020 North Water Street is primarily remembered in Bay City's history as being the Campbell House Hotel. The 125,000-square-foot building served as an office and retail center before the hotel was established in 1868. The hotel changed owners and, in 1920, was converted from a hotel into two separate businesses, Sams Brothers and Co. (a grocery store) and Robinson Brothers Clothing. C.E. Rosenbury and Sons bought out the grocery store and turned that portion of the building into a furniture store. The clothing store continued to remain in business until 1931, when Rosenbury's Furniture claimed full use of the building. For fifty-four years, the furniture store remained in business until it was bought out by Bill and Elaine Fournier, who have created the largest and most impressive antique mall in the region. The mall features antiques from all over the world from all different periods.

Since before the Fourniers came into ownership of the building, people had been having unexplainable occurrences in the building, often reporting their spooky experiences to the couple. "Rosenbury's employees told us that they would be all closed down for the night, ready to leave and would hear footsteps upstairs. When they went to locate what they presumed was an errant shopper, there would be no one there." Elaine also reported some strange happenings in the basement of the center: "There were offices in the basement of the building and several times when employees had arrived at work in the morning, papers would be all over the place, despite things being in good order the night before." Elaine recalled one experience that had totally spooked her two teenage children when she first began working in the building. "Often, we would work very late into the evening. There was an intercom system throughout the store which was left up by the previous owners. The kids would turn on the intercom that monitored the second floor and listen. They reported hearing all sorts of noises." She revealed that based on what her son had heard on the intercom, he refused to enter the second floor at night without his German shepherd by his side. When Elaine inquired about his fear of the second floor, he explained to his mother that he had felt something pass through him.

The Bay City Antiques Center is located at the intersection of Third and Water Streets in downtown Bay City. *Author photo*.

The second floor of the Bay City Antiques Center has many reported claims of paranormal activity. *Author photo*.

One local resident reported an alarming incident on the second floor of the center that she has not been able to explain. It was a rainy September afternoon, and the downtown area was nearly deserted. Ashley Harris wandered into the antique shop looking to add to her collection of old records. She felt as though she hit the lottery. "No one was in the store except for me and two employees. Water Street was like a ghost town. I was super happy it was a slow day at the Antiques Center. I felt like I could really take my time sorting through the old music with no distractions." As she wandered through the different vendor booths, keeping her eyes open for anything that caught her attention, she eventually made her way upstairs, where she spotted an entire bin of vinyl. As she excitedly thumbed through the crate, an eerie feeling overcame her. "I remember experiencing this intense feeling that I was being watched. My hair was standing on end." She slowly turned around and did not see anyone, so despite her discomfort, she brushed it off as nonsense and returned to her search. About a minute later, she was interrupted by the sound of high-heeled shoes on the wooden floor. "It sounded like someone was getting closer and closer to me. I felt very confused. I did not recall seeing anyone up on that floor, and I couldn't pinpoint where the sound was coming from." Ashley made her way to the center of the room looking for any sign of life when suddenly she heard a woman faintly whispering inside the storage room of doors off to her right. Upon turning toward the sound, her eyes met with the figure of a lady who appeared to be from the Victorian era. She was clad in a lacy purple dress and tall black laced-up boots, with her brown hair in an updo. "Her eyes were black, and her face was ashen. It was like she was staring into my soul, her eyes almost glowing from beyond the darkness of her eye sockets and her bruised lips curled up into an unsettling grin." Ashley stood there in a state of shock, unable to stop her body from trembling as she watched the figure slowly take a step closer and beckon Ashley with her pointer finger before vanishing into thin air. "I dropped the records I was holding. I could not breathe. It was like all the air had left my lungs." Ashley remembered briskly exiting the upper level and walking out of the store. "The staff told me to have a nice day, and I couldn't even respond to them. I probably seemed like a jerk." Ashley stated that when she told others of her experience, she was met with hostility. "I know what I saw. People can think whatever they want. I know for certain that what I saw was an actual ghost. I haven't slept with the lights off since."

Harold Beauchamp Jr., another local resident and paranormal enthusiast, experienced his own chilling encounter on the main floor of the center. As

The location on the second level of the Bay City Antiques Center where a sinister-looking Victorian woman has been spotted. *Author photo.*

a proud retired U.S. Marine Corps veteran, Harold frequently visited the antique center on the hunt for rare military memorabilia. One morning while out with his wife, they decided to stop by the store to look around. While browsing the displays, Harold had discovered a vintage marine's visor hat from World War II. Looking at the heathered olive cap with black bill and equally striking black USMC emblem pin attached, Harold was transfixed. "I'm a hat collector, so it was really neat to find something like this. Especially in such great condition!" Without hesitation, he clutched the hat between his fingers and made his way over to the north end of the store toward the kitchen furnishings, where he followed the distinct odor of a homemade meal cooking. As he passed through the room of dining tables and old stoves, it smelled as if someone was making a pot roast complete with warm tomato soup and mashed potatoes. The smell dissipated within an instant. Wandering through the numerous antique treasures, Harold heard a whisper in his left ear, "Hey, what are you doing with that hat?" After the jolt of surprise, he suddenly relaxed when he recognized it to be the voice of a woman. "Ellen, you won't believe what year this is from!" He proceeded to speak with his wife as he continued meandering throughout the booths, gazing on the relics of a bygone era. As he finally turned to show his wife the hat, no one was there, even though just seconds earlier he was talking to

An area on the first floor of the Bay City Antiques Center where people have reported the phantom smell of home cooking. *Author photo.*

someone. But who? As he stood there in confusion, the whispery voice came again from directly behind him. "I'm right here." At this exact moment, from the opposite end of the room, Ellen came strolling in: "I was looking for you. I have to show you something I think my sister might like for Christmas." Harold looked around and discovered that no one else was there with him, "Elly, was that you just talking to me?" he asked suspiciously. Ellen gave him a strange look. "No. I was looking at purses. I was not anywhere near you. You know that." After believing that the military cap had some type of attachment, Harold set it down before exiting the store with the intention of not wanting to disturb whoever or whatever remained connected to it.

With so many dated artifacts in one location, there is an energy within the building that is unlike any other. The Antiques Center is a staple within Bay City's downtown area, and people have come from far and wide to discover its charm. To the unappreciative mind, the center is just another building of brick and wood, but it is alive with the memories of many and has been a witness to the beauty and atrocities of the city's dramatic past.

3

SPECTERS AND STORYBOOKS

Heavy footsteps following your every step, full-bodied apparitions and books being strewn across the floors without ever being touched by human hands. This sounds like something straight out of Hollywood, but alas these incidents have been reported by staff and patrons of the Sage Public Library for over a century. Shrouded by trees, just steps away from the Midland Street Historic District, stands the iconic library of Bay City's West Side. This intricately detailed red-brick building of Victorian Gothic, French Chateau and Ruskin Gothic architecture is an exquisite structure that dominates the area with its unsurpassed beauty. It greets visitors up the concrete stairwell with an elegant cast-iron fountain portraying Leda and the Swan, a story from Greek mythology. Residing in an alcove on the anterior portion of the building is a terra-cotta figure called the *Lady of Learning*. Her purpose is to lead people, particularly children, to the library to encourage a love of reading and scientific research. Inside, the building has elements of a distant time when people took pride in workmanship and the longevity of what they constructed. You can find little clues into the building's origins and past by the fine details throughout the interior, such as endearing painted tiles representing fairytales from England surrounding the face of the fireplace, a red lantern bearing the Sage namesake and a Koberger Bible dating back to the year 1492—gifted by a German immigrant in 1900—that is now hidden deep within the library's vault. Sage is the oldest library still in use in not only the city but also the entire state of Michigan. It was gifted by lumber baron Henry

The *Lady of Learning* in front of Sage Library promoting a love of reading and scientific research. *Courtesy of Mary Ruthko, Bay County Library System.*

Sage to the citizens of West Bay City, what was then called the Village of West Wenona, in January 1884.

On January 31, 1814, in Middletown, Connecticut, Sally and Charles Sage gave birth to their first child, Henry Williams Sage. Prior to his family relocating to Ithaca, New York, Henry attended a school in Bristol, Connecticut. He had initially aspired for a career in medicine and in 1830 was training under Dr. Austin Church, but oddly enough, due to unforeseen health issues, he could not continue pursuing his education. Despite this unfortunate time in his life, Henry kept his eye on the prize of a life of success and comfort. Two years later, Henry Sage was offered a position as a clerk in his maternal uncles' mercantile business, Williams & Brothers. It was in this role that he had discovered he had a real talent for the business industry and was flourishing as an entrepreneur. Henry was proud of his growing accomplishments, as he feared he would end up like his father. As Henry grew older, he viewed his father as a failure because Charles's business endeavors always resulted in disappointment. His father's string of bad luck had motivated him to work as hard as he could to build a life of promise for himself. In 1837, Henry's determination and diligent work ethic was rewarded with a huge promotion, and he took over ownership of the family business. For the next twenty years, Henry Sage continued to develop in his role as owner and earned a reputation in Ithaca as one of the top business tycoons in the city. Deep down, though, Henry had always desired to start his own company and be a self-made man. Sage had discovered how profitable the lumbering industry was becoming and, in 1854, invested some of his funds in building a lumbering factory on Lake Simcoe in Ontario, Canada. Ten years later, Henry Sage partnered with another fellow lumberman from New York by the name of John McGraw, and together they built the largest lumbering mill in the entire world at that time. This massive mill, known as the Sage, McGraw & Company sawmill,

Sage Lumber Mill and Yards at Bay City Michigan. Original painting in the possession of Mrs. Henry M. Sage, Menands Road, Albany, New York. *Photographed by Lois A. (Mrs. Henry) Merrill, Loundonville, New York, January 21, 1956. Collection of Regional History, Cornell University, Division of Rare and Manuscript Collections.*

was located where Veteran's Memorial Park stands today. Thus, Sage became a significant pioneer in the history of West Bay City. In 1882, the mill was producing upward of thirty-one million feet of lumber.

The mill encouraged population growth on the west side of the city, and in 1863, Henry Sage proposed to name the expanding village Lake City. Upon discovering that there was already a city in Michigan with the same name, Sage decided on the name Wenona after Hiawatha's beautiful mother in the poem penned by Henry Wadsworth Longfellow. If you drive down the streets of West Bay City today, you will notice many of the streets are named after people, many of whom were members of both Sage's and McGraw's families. Sadly, there is no Charles Street in honor of Henry Sage's father. Sage eventually purchased full ownership of the business from John McGraw in 1868, and the business remained thriving until 1885. The timberlands were becoming bare, so Sage began to invest in pinelands, which eventually met the same fate as the timberlands. Given the reduced resources, Henry Sage decided to shut down his operation once and for all.

Sage was grateful for how well the citizens of Wenona received him and wanted to leave them something behind as a token of his appreciation. As someone who had a deep love for education, he thought it best to leave behind something other than a sawmill that could be utilized by the public. Sage was so ahead of his time when it came to his beliefs on learning that he even believed women deserved the same educational opportunities as men did, which was almost unheard of in that era. This newfangled way of thinking was demonstrated when he moved to Brooklyn, New York, and attended the very first graduation ceremony at Cornell University. It was at this ceremony that Henry presented his lifelong friend Ezra Cornell, the university's co-founder, with the idea of constructing a college just for women. Henry was viewed as a philanthropic man with a soft spot for women and children in his heart. In the city that he had created, he desired to build an intellectual and proper social society and devised the idea of gifting

Henry Williams Sage. *Courtesy of Cornell University Library, Division of Rare and Manuscript Collections.*

a library to the city. On January 16, 1884, this idea became a reality. Sage donated the land and ten thousand books to the city in order to create the Sage Public Library. It is believed that the library cost upward of $50,000 to erect. Contrary to rumors, Sage Library never served as a home to Henry Sage. However, the basement of the building was briefly used as a school, while the third floor was where the school administration offices were located. In 1980, the library was listed on the National Register of Historic Places. Despite several renovations and the age of the building, the Bay County Library System has done an excellent job of maintaining the library for generations to come.

While Sage was indeed a generous man, some of his workers felt otherwise. It has been rumored that Sage used some of his employees' funds in the construction of the building. Legend goes that Sage's disgruntled workers roam the multifloored library in spirit form demanding their hard-earned money back. Staff have reported eerie happenings late in the evenings when alone in the locked building. There have been multiple reports of staff being followed by something that cannot be seen. One employee, who wished to remain anonymous, stated, "I had just finished locking the front doors and was doing one more round in the building to make sure everything was in order, when I heard what sounded like heavy boots stomping behind me. I checked everything out and I didn't see anyone." With fearful eyes, she continued,

I was creeped out but made it my goal to finish my work quickly so I could get out of there as soon as possible. When I descended the stairwell and got to the landing, I heard the thudding of the boots coming down the stairs after me. All I could do was freeze in terror and gaze upward at the upper levels, praying I wouldn't come face to face with whoever was making all that noise.

Other employees who have had opening shifts have reported walking into chaos in the morning, with the library in fine condition the night prior. "Some books were arranged in strange patterns and placed neatly across the room from where they should have been, while others were in disarray all over the floor as if they were caught in a windstorm."

Possibly one of the most depressing stories, and unsettling to those who have seen her, is the spirit of the little girl who is said to haunt the third floor. Guests and employees alike have reported seeing this child ghost for over one hundred years. She is believed to be younger than ten years old, has a disfigured complexion and is seen wearing a long white dress. In a letter dated June 18, 1901, received by the library of West Bay City, Miss M.E. Ahern addresses the issue of a small child who died by contracting smallpox from a library book. Ahern goes on to say that she did not know of any

Sage Library around the time it was gifted to West Bay City in 1884. *Courtesy of Mary Ruthko, Bay County Library System.*

library that had a smallpox epidemic but that she was "very much grieved to hear of little Miss Burns being a victim of the dreadful malady."

On November 23, 2013, the Tri-City Ghost Hunters Society had the opportunity to check out these claims of activity and made a historical discovery of one individual who remains attached to the building. The investigation began in the attic where Ellen Beauchamp and a few other female investigators were present. After climbing the drop-down stairwell to the attic and entering the room, Ellen turned on her spirit box with the hopes of connecting with the ghostly little girl that so many others have reported in the building. However, the child spirit did not make her presence known that night; instead, it was a male spirit. When she asked the spirit to reveal its name, Ellen was able to document a masculine voice stating, "Jacob." When another investigator asked again, "Could you tell us your name?" the voice answered promptly, "I just did." Thinking that perhaps there was a fluke with the equipment, Ellen asked again, "Could you tell us the name of a person who is here with us right now?" This time, a woman responded with the hurried but distinct name of "Jacob." A few days after the investigation, the society contacted the managing librarian of Sage Public Library, Kirsten Grantham-Wellnitz, for answers on who Jacob may have been. Kirsten informed the society that according to past board records, in 1904 and 1906, a Jacob Beck was paid to lay and clean the carpet. According to old Bay City directories, there was indeed a prominent carpenter by the name of Jacob Beck in Bay City who operated J Beck & Son (Jacob and Jacob Jr.) Steam Carpet Cleaning Works, and his business was located at 518 North Lincoln Avenue. According to historical records, this is the only Jacob hired to work at the Sage Public Library who has since passed away. The transcriptions from the 1904 and 1906 board minutes of the Sage Library revealed that Jacob Beck Sr. was paid $11.36 for both cleaning and laying the carpet, and in 1906, he was compensated $5.18 for cleaning the carpet. After weeks of digging and some help from Mark Grotelueschen, head of reference services at the Alice and Jack Wirt Public Library, Tri-City Ghost Hunters Society was finally able to locate Jacob Beck Sr.'s obituary and discovered that much like Henry Sage, Jacob Beck Sr. was a pioneer of Bay City. On April 12, 1909, at 2:00 a.m., Jacob Beck Sr. died at the age of seventy-one after a stroke of paralysis. He had arrived in Bay City in 1868 and was well known throughout the county, especially in the German community, for being of strong moral character. He was a member of both the German Evangelical Lutheran Church and the Arbeiter Society. At the time of his death, he left behind five daughters and four sons, one of whom he ran his carpeting

Sage Library is the oldest continually operated library in the state of Michigan. *Courtesy of Mary Ruthko, Bay County Library System.*

business with. A few mediums who visited the library years prior to the Tri-City Ghost Hunters Society stated that there was a man in the building that was particular about the carpet and he chose to remain at Sage in order to ensure his hard work was being maintained.

The stories and legends surrounding the Sage Public Library will continue to live on. This architectural masterpiece has stood the test of time and so have its specters. On your next visit, make sure to pull up a chair, grab a good book and stay awhile. There are a few spirits who have been dying to meet you.

4

THE RITE MAN OF THE MASONIC

The posh-looking tan brick building facing East Center Avenue is not home to a secret society but rather a society with secrets. The Scottish Rite Masonic Center, home to the Valley of Bay City, is an appendant body of the world's oldest and largest fraternity in the world, the Freemasons. The Freemasons' mission has always been to help make good men better and to help them be a positive influence for their families and communities. As an appendant body, the Scottish Rite is an avenue for brothers of the fraternity to "seek further light" after obtaining the degree of master Mason. The Scottish Rite is one of the more popular associated organizations of the Masonic Fraternity. In 1925, the Scottish Rite Masonic Center building was built adjacent to the original temple, the meeting place at the time for several area lodges. Due to the immense popularity of the Scottish Rite, it quickly started to outgrow the space needed for Scottish Rite activities. The Valley of Bay City covers a geographical area just south of the Mackinaw Bridge, as far west as Alma, to Genesee County and out to the Thumb. With the substantial number of Scottish Rite Masons, the property adjacent to the Masonic temple was purchased and ground was broken. Little did the brothers know that these two historic buildings would be a playground for an army of the dead.

In 1874, the original Masonic temple bordering Sixth Street and North Madison Avenue was chartered and finally built on a foundation of dolomitic limestone in 1893. The red Richardsonian Romanesque design of Rock River brownstone with elegant Moorish Revival embellishments, stained-

Masons gathering outside of the original Masonic temple. *Courtesy of the Bay City Scottish Rite Masonic Center.*

glass windows, onion-domed rooftop and a 114-foot copper-domed bell tower, made the Masonic one of the most opulent structures in the entirety of Michigan. This masterpiece was the creation of local architects Leverett Pratt and Walter Koeppe, who designed many other outstanding buildings within the city, such as St. Stanislaus Church, Bay City Hall, the LaPorte Building, the Webster House Bed and Breakfast, First Presbyterian Church and the Crapo Building, along with many others.

Unfortunately, in the spring of 1903, only ten years after it was built, the temple caught fire and its beautiful and unique elements were destroyed. The loss of this majestic piece of art was devastating. The copper recovered from the site of destruction was further melted down and turned into coins as a remembrance of the building's former splendor. It was then gifted to the local Joppa Lodge Masons. These coins can be seen on display today within the building. Two years later, in 1905, the Masonic temple was rebuilt in a much simpler fashion with fire-resistant elements. The once beautiful onion-domed rooftop was ultimately replaced with heavy steel. As the lumbering industry began to dwindle and the automobile industry began to flourish, Bay City fell on hard times. The economy was doing so poorly that city officials had abandoned the town in order to pursue

Illustration of Bay City Masonic Temple, circa 1898. *University of Michigan Bentley Historical Library.*

more lucrative ventures. The Freemasons were not immune to the slowing economy. Down to only one lodge, Joppa Lodge, residing in the building, struggling to provide regular philanthropic deeds to the community, it was no longer as financially feasible to remain open. The funds needed to operate and maintain such a grand facility, as well as other Masonic temples throughout the state, were beginning to diminish. Finally, in 2004, a big decision had to be made. Joppa Lodge had to decide whether to find a group that would take on the laborious task of preserving the building or demolish it by wrecking ball. With heavy hearts, the Masons had decided to take the route of demolishing the building.

One local organization, the Bay Arts Council, could not bear the thought of losing a structure of such grandiosity, and in 2005, an agreement was made so that the Bay Arts Council could promptly begin much needed historical renovations and fundraising endeavors. A nonprofit group, the Friends of the Historic Masonic Temple of Bay City, dedicated to the temple's historic preservation, took ownership from the Bay Arts Council. The building no longer serves Joppa Lodge Masons anymore, but it's still Masonic in spirit. With an attachment to the newer Scottish Rite center by a hallway that runs longitudinally, how could it not be?

The Freemasons have a complex organization to understand with its varying levels of membership and chapters. The Scottish Rite, as previously stated, is an appendant body of Masonic fraternity. Once someone has completed three degrees of symbolic Masonry, obtained in what is informally called "Blue Lodge," the Scottish Rite is seen as a continuation of "Masonic education," offering twenty-nine additional degrees, from the fourth to the thirty-second degree. The Scottish Rite also has the thirty-third degree, which is an honorary degree and cannot be applied for, as it must be earned. Despite contrary belief, the term *Scottish* does not have anything to do with originating in Scotland. It is actually derived from the French word *Ecossais*, which means Scottish. It has always been incorrectly assumed that Freemasonry is a religion-based organization. However, it is true that in order to be a member within the society, you must hold some belief in a monotheistic God.

The Scottish Rite Center, while not as intricate on the outside of the building as the historic Masonic temple, is still a foundation of beauty in its own right. The building looms over Bay City's wealthiest street like a towering sanctuary. Designed by Grand Rapids architects Osgood and Osgood, the fifteenth-century English Perpendicular–style consistory with wooden front doors and an overhead hanging lantern give one the impression of stepping back in time. Inside the center, you can find many lavish rooms all over the building, the most notable being the cathedral-like theater and a vintage barbershop. The facility is often used today as a wedding venue.

One specific bride recalled sitting in the barbershop, also referred to as the costume room or bridal suite. With her immaculate hair and makeup, she finally slipped into her sparkling white gown and was filled to the brim with joy. She just could not wait to marry the man of her dreams. Here she was in this stunning building anxiously excited to utter the words, "I do," when she noticed an older gentleman in a suit and glasses standing in the darkened tunnel that abuts the bridal suite. She walked up to him curiously, as she had not seen him before and hoped everything was scheduled to go as planned. "Is everything ok?" she asked. He looked at her with adoring eyes and smiled sweetly. "Oh, darling," he began, "you look positively beautiful." The bride swelled with pride at the compliment and was just about to thank him when he disappeared before her eyes.

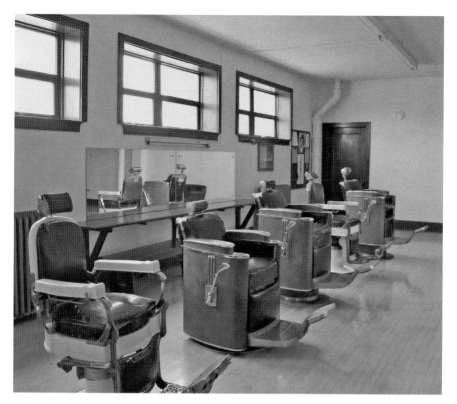

The barbershop at the Scottish Rite Masonic Center where the ghost of Charles E. Sharp is often spotted. *Courtesy of Kristen Sanborn.*

There she stood wide eyed with wonder; this figure as solid as herself had vanished into thin air. These strange sightings began when Charles E. Sharp, the center's secretary of thirty-six years and a thirty-third-degree member of the Scottish Rite, passed away in 1967. In fact, to this day, many brides who have had their weddings at the Scottish Rite Center have claimed to see the man in the tunnel eagerly awaiting the opportunity to build up these brides on their special day. Chris Sova, current executive secretary, has experienced many reported sightings of Sharp as well.

Chris's desire to become a Mason was motivated by the idea of participating in charitable affairs within the community. Chris is a member of Joppa Lodge and joined the Scottish Rite shortly after becoming a master Mason. It was not long until Chris discovered the presence of Charlie. Chris has reported seeing the lower portion of a man's body clad in a business suit throughout the six-story building on multiple occasions. "I have yet to see a

Left: M. Charles E. Sharp, 33°, M.S., Secretary, Bay City Scottish Rite Bodies, July 1, 1931–July 1, 1967. *Courtesy of the Bay City Scottish Rite Masonic Center.*

Below: The auditorium of the Scottish Rite Masonic Center, where self-luminating spheres have been witnessed. *Courtesy of Kristen Sanborn.*

full-bodied apparition of Charlie, but many brides who've gotten married here have. Every time I've witnessed him, it was always just the lower half of his body, with a torso or a leg manifesting first." The auditorium seems to be a portal of paranormal activity, with frequent occurrences of what Chris has referred to as "zooming." With Chris being such an active member of the fraternity, he often spends a substantial amount of time alone in the building. On multiple occasions, whenever he entered the auditorium, he would see something glowing in his peripheral vision. As he turned to see what the light source was, he saw self-luminating spheres that were larger than a softball darting throughout the auditorium. "I'm a nurse by profession, so I initially thought maybe something was wrong with my eyes. Based on what I've seen, I do believe these experiences I've had to be paranormal." Chris claimed that the incidents have made him so uneasy, he has started to turn on the lights when he walks through the building at night. "The experiences here have genuinely spooked me," he confessed.

Anyone starting a new position can relate to the anxiety that comes with navigating unfamiliar territories and new responsibilities, but what about if you also had to deal with something you could not see? The Great Lakes Bay Region Children's Dyslexia Center located on the fifth floor of the Scottish Rite building was looking to fulfill a position. The center's director, Nancy Williams, has the first words uttered to her on her first day on the job etched in her memory. "If you're here alone late at night and you hear something, just say hello to Charlie and everything will be just fine." One can imagine how unnerving it must have been on her first night alone, locked inside, when she heard the roaring sound of furniture moving around in the dining room below her. On numerous occasions, she heard furniture being rearranged and people making a ruckus, only to realize that she was still alone. Despite the commotion, she always said hello to Charlie, in hopes of ceasing the activity. She began using the sixth floor, the building's old poker room, as a storage facility. She found it spacious and conveniently secluded from the rest of the center since it could not be accessed by elevator. The attic can only be accessed by passing through a single door on the fifth floor and climbing one flight of stairs in the back corner of the building. Regularly, when Nancy was alone and working nearby the stairwell to the attic, she heard boxes shuffling around above her. "The only items up there are mine, and there is only one access point to get up there. There's no reason for anyone to be in there, and even if someone were there, they would have passed me on the way up."

Possibly one of the creepiest paranormal stories in relation to the structure, is that of Chris's young daughter, who, on every visit to the center, has waved and said hello toward a small door leading to the pipe organ. The door leads to different levels up ladders and through doorways. Is something or someone hiding inside? It is possible, but we may never know.

The adjoined historic Masonic temple also has its fair share of paranormal activity. In fact, Nick Suchyta, director of Bay City's nonprofit Masonic temple preservation group, stated, "I was a skeptic until I started working here." Nick working graveyard shifts at the temple really awakened the spirits. Surely most people who work long hours enjoy listening to music to make the time pass as quickly as possible, but Nick has gained another reason to appreciate music. "I have to play it to drown out the voices. I hear male and female voices conversing all night long." Unfortunately, that is not the only nuisance Nick has dealt with from those within the supernatural realm. "Doors unlock that I definitely know I locked. I will go set something down for a second, come back and it is wide open. It's left me and the other volunteers totally puzzled." Of course, Charlie makes his rounds through the Masonic temple as well.

Gary Conklin, a member of Joppa Lodge who regularly cleaned the Masonic temple when the lodge owned the building, was about to head into the game room to tidy up when he discovered that on the other side of the door was a scene straight out of the 1930s. As Gary watched the memories of the past play out before his very eyes, he took in the amazing amount of detail that he was seeing. There was a group of gentlemen dressed in their Sunday best, sitting, smoking, laughing and talking. Gary blinked hard in disbelief, and the room was empty. Within an instant, the impressive vision was gone, and Gary was a changed man by the experience. As he approached Chris with the famous words, "You're never going to believe me, but…" Chris already had an inkling of what he was going to say. I guess it is true what they say, "Once a Mason, always a Mason," even in death.

A well-dressed older man is the most common figure reported by visitors and volunteers. Along with Charlie, a bizarre-looking young female spirit has also been spotted, primarily in the Purple Room and the Club Room. Johna Shorey, a local paranormal investigator, was volunteering at one of the temple's haunted attractions when she realized she was no longer in her designated spot alone. At first thinking it was another volunteer in costume, Johna paid the girl no mind, but on closer inspection, she perceived something was not quite right. "I spotted a girl around twelve years old or so. She was just standing there, looking reminiscent of Samara from *The Ring*, blending in with the corner of the room. Her long black hair was draped over her face as she hung her head and her arms were hanging limply at

One of the best-kept secrets that the Masonic buildings share is that they both sit atop the old site of a cemetery. You can see the since-demolished church standing alongside both buildings in this aerial photograph. *Courtesy of the Bay City Scottish Rite Masonic Center.*

her sides. She was creepy." The Friends of the Historic Masonic Temple's treasurer, Kelley Kent, has encountered another female entity that appeared a lot less intimidating. As Kelley was preparing one evening for the haunted Masonic temple fundraising event, she was ascending the staircase to the billiards room to get some supplies when she spotted a girl from about eight to twelve years old peeking out at her from behind the bannister of the stairwell. Kelley recalled her having a short blond bobbed haircut and wearing a blousy white shirt with a plaid skirt and Mary Jane–style shoes with long stockings. "When she saw me, she flattened herself against the wall and looked at me wide eyed. As soon as I went to speak to her, she was just gone." Kelley further stated that this young girl did not fit the appearance of anyone else who had been volunteering for the event. "I couldn't pinpoint the year that she was from, but her clothing was definitely dated." Various other disappearing figures have been reported in the Masonic temple as well. A preschool-aged girl with brown hair, a middle-aged man that enjoys chain-smoking cigars and sports a top hat and an elegant young woman with long golden hair cascading down her flowy violet dress are some of the additional figures spotted by volunteers and locals around the building.

One of the best-kept secrets that these Masonic buildings share is that both the Scottish Rite Masonic Center and Historic Masonic Temple sit atop the site of an old cemetery. Before the Scottish Rite Center was constructed, it is believed that the bodies were exhumed and taken to Oak Ridge Cemetery. Could their souls have been left behind to wander the many halls for all eternity? The buildings remain a hotbed of ghostly happenings, so it's entirely possible. Just remember that if you visit, do not leave without saying hello to Charlie first.

5
SHEARER TERROR

In every city, there are a few buildings that are iconic. These places have stood the test of time, and although different businesses have moved in and out over the years, the structures continue to thrive. In Bay City, the Shearer Brothers Building is one of those kinds of places. It is used today for residential and commercial purposes and by day sits amid the chaotic rush of Bay City's downtown area. At night, however, the building, along with the block it sits on, becomes an entirely different place. A spooky place.

James Shearer, the building's architect, was born in Albany, New York, on July 12, 1823, to Scottish parents George Shearer and Agnes Buchanan. James's parents were affluent farmers who worked extremely hard. They were loving, kind and honest people who cared deeply about the future of their four children. Sadly, an unfortunate fire destroyed their property and left the family in financial ruin. Although the children could no longer get the prestigious education their parents intended them to have, their parents ensured that they at least received a basic education with the hopes of giving them an advantage in life. James Shearer, determined to change his own fate, found employment at a store within his hometown and worked there for two years until he realized he needed more of a challenge. Everyone around him observed his sharp, studious and mathematical mind and knew he was destined for something greater. On May 1838, at only fifteen years old, James traveled to Detroit to pursue a more successful life. This part of the United States was still relatively new at the time, and James believed that moving west would be more beneficial to him than anything the East

The Shearer Brothers Building, 2019. *Author photo.*

Coast had to offer. For the next six years, he committed himself to an apprenticeship with a building. During that time, he studied geometry and architecture religiously, with the goal of becoming an engineer. Shearer had definitely found his passion in the building trades.

In order to further his education, in 1844, James returned to New York to attend the Albany Academy. However, after just one semester, he again wanted to pursue permanent employment. In the fall of 1845, he moved to Montgomery, Alabama, where he began working on the construction of the new capitol. He was so well educated and a natural at his craft that he was promoted to be the project's superintendent. However, in 1847, James was still not satisfied with his lot in life and once again headed to Detroit to fulfill his destiny. It was in Detroit that he became a successful businessman by deciding to establish his own engineering and construction firm. Things were going well for James, and during this peak of success, he married the love of his life, Margaret Hutchinson, in May 1850.

James had soon earned a reputation in Detroit as one of the most accomplished builders in the entire city. In 1859, he was selected to join a commission and given the authority to choose the design of Detroit's city hall. In 1861, he was elected as an alderman in the city of Detroit. One of his duties included providing soldiers from Michigan to assist the Union in the

Civil War. Until 1865, James and Margaret lived happily in Detroit, where they had built a family with three sons and a daughter. During his time in Detroit, James had heard about the success of the lumbering industry in Bay City and decided to visit in hopes of learning more about the trade. After his visit, James purchased the Raymond Sawmill, located at the end of Water Street on Bay City's East Side. He then hired his brother George to run the mill. James decided that he wanted to be part of the exciting lumbering boom and took up his final residence in Bay City.

Upon his arrival, he found immediate success and was well received within the city. He quickly got to work by building the first brick dwelling at 701 Center Avenue, where he lived with his family, in addition to the first sewers within the city. He was a busy man and appointed to many organizations during this time. He became the first president of the Lumberman's Association of the Saginaw Valley and Bay City's water works board, as well as the president of the First National Bank, which he served from 1867 to 1881. Other honorary positions he held included member of the University of Michigan board of regents for eight years, trustee of the public library and trustee of the First Presbyterian Church for fifteen years. During his wide-reaching community involvement, he operated businesses in the banking, building, real estate and lumber industries. To say he was a busy man would be an understatement.

James Shearer had built a trio of blocks in the downtown Bay City area during his lifetime. He erected his first business block in 1866. It was called the Shearer block, located on the corner of Water Street and Center Avenue, directly across from the Delta Planetarium. Today, a few of the businesses that operate on this block are the Mill End Lofts and Tavern 101. Shearer's architectural style is striking; everything he designed is perfectly symmetrical. The home he built at 701 Center Avenue is still standing today and is a perfect example of his precision. It is said if the home was cut directly down the center from the front doors, each half would look identical to the other. James favored a Second Empire architectural style, first introduced in France during Napoleon III's reign. Shearer impressed those within his trade by being extremely hardworking and someone who took absolute pride in his work. He desired to build locations that would last for generations. He was known within the industry to use only the highest-quality materials during construction. In 1871, prior to Shearer building his second block, the governor of Michigan, Henry P. Baldwin, chose Shearer as one of only three commissioners to oversee construction of Lansing's capitol building. Once that task had been completed, James continued onward with his projects. In 1880, James completed the Shearer Central block, which is located on the corner of Center and Washington Avenues. The last and final block he built was called the Shearer Brothers block, located on the corner of Center Avenue and Adams Street. The building was completed in 1884 and served as an office building. It has since been renovated with condominiums on the upper level and small businesses at the street level. On October 14, 1896, James Shearer passed away in the beautiful brick home he had built and shared with his wife.

Much like James Shearer, Justin Rodriguez is an extremely motivated and hardworking person, so it was only natural that he was drawn to the Shearer Brothers Building to turn one of his dreams into a reality. When Justin rented out the space at 809 Adams Street to launch another one of his businesses, the last thing he and his family expected to encounter were ghosts. Justin, owner of Voodoo Tattoo, is a gifted, artistic and savvy businessman. His wife and business partner/manager, Shannon, is also an exceptionally talented individual who creates handbags and period costumes in addition to running a handmade candle business. Together they decided that they had wanted to

The home built by James Shearer, at 701 Center Avenue, showcases his precision. The home is currently used for apartments. *Author photo.*

To the immediate left of the circular business sign is where the Belle Epoque Art Gallerie once operated. *Author photo.*

create an artists' guild in Bay City. The Belle Epoque Art Gallerie was born in 2007, and it was established as a place for anyone with a love of the arts to hang out, paint, participate in poetry slams and engage in anything else that would encourage the use of one's imagination. The term *belle epoque* is a French phrase meaning "beautiful era."

Historically speaking, the Belle Époque (1871–1914) was an incredibly positive time in history. It was known as a peaceful and prosperous time. Justin and Shannon had hopes of bringing the citizens of Bay City the ability to enjoy elements of the past by visiting their art gallery, thus naming their endeavor after a time in history they believed to be stunning and socially charming. They even intended to open an absinthe bar so people could enjoy the traditional drink of many historic creators.

As absinthe has an extremely high alcohol content (usually 90 to 160 proof), the drink puts anyone brave enough to finish a glass into a state of euphoria. In fact, absinthe used to have such a high content of thujone, an element of wormwood, that individuals hallucinated after drinking it. Because of its hallucinogenic reputation and strength, between 1910 and

1915, absinthe was deemed illegal in most countries. Of course, in 2007, the United States decided to regulate the amount of thujone in the liquor and stated that it was allowed to contain only ten milligrams of thujone per liter, unlike the thirty-five milligrams per liter that Europe allowed. It was an extremely popular drink among nineteenth-century scholars, artists, writers and poets, as it was said to boost one's creativity and foster artistic expression. Legends like Picasso, Edgar Allan Poe, Van Gogh and Hemingway frequently enjoyed absinthe for its many unique qualities. The bright green liquor, often referred to as the "Green Fairy," is traditionally served by melting a sugar cube over a slotted spoon. Traditional absinthe tends to be a bitter black licorice–flavored drink made with wormwood, anise and fennel, while other types of absinthe contain flowers and herbs. Across the world, absinthe varies by color and flavor. Unfortunately, as cool as it would have been to bring this rare and notable drink to Bay City's downtown area, Justin and Shannon struggled greatly with getting a liquor license, as the city has strict limits. If you would like to try this special drink, you'll have to make a special drive to The Whitney in Detroit or the Mad Hatter Café and Bistro in Birmingham, Michigan.

Despite not getting the liquor license, Shannon and Justin perfected their studio with a gothic Victorian theme. The walls were painted a deep maroon red, the doorways featured black trim and the ceiling was a harvest golden color. Masterpieces created by local Bay City artists graced the walls, including some of Justin's own paintings. Vintage furniture, frames and an antique fireplace completed the look. When you stepped into the Belle Epoque Art Gallerie, it was as if a time travel machine had whisked you up and dropped you into another century. It was clever, it was elegant and it was memorable. It was unlike any other location in Bay City. When you entered the front door of the gallery, you were greeted into a large room with art-filled walls and a dark, yet romantic atmosphere. If you wandered straight back, before reaching the bathroom you would pass through a small room with a few chairs. From the bathroom, which was the farthest room in the gallery's entrance, you could access the basement, which contained accessible underground tunnels. Shannon recalled them being narrow and ominous. She was able to travel from Adams Street to the intersection of Center and Madison Avenues before she discovered a dead end. "The pitch blackness inside the tunnels was unnerving, and it was difficult to navigate through. I don't know how people in the past managed," One of the biggest issues at Belle Epoque Art Gallerie was keeping the basement door closed. The door latched just fine and

Remnants of the underground tunnels of Bay City. *Author photo.*

was locked up every evening during close, but every morning when the Rodriguezes came in, it was like someone had left the door wide open. The door was huge and made of heavy lumber. How it opened so easily despite being leaden and latched continues to be a mystery.

Although the basement had some activity, the room that always made Shannon feel the most uneasy was the small room right before the bathroom. She stated that within that room, she always had the feeling that she was being watched by something. She never experienced any apparition sightings in this part of the building, but she knew that she was not alone. Sure enough, Shannon eventually had her own paranormal sighting at the Belle Epoque Art Gallerie in November 2009, a month before it closed for good.

On a snowy fall evening long after the gallery had closed for the day, Shannon and Justin had decided to have a small gathering with friends at the gallery after hours, as they often did. Shannon and her friend Jake were sitting near the window and watching the snowfall as they both caught up with each other and enjoyed listening to the music playing in the background. As they were getting lost in conversation, Shannon asked Jake nonchalantly, "Hey, is it still snowing out there?" They both looked out the window at the same time and saw two people standing outside the window just staring back at them, not moving. Shannon squinted and leaned forward to get a closer look at the pair, which appeared to be a man and a woman. Adams Street was glowing by streetlights, and though these figures appeared as darkened shadows, Shannon recognized the clothing the people were wearing, despite never having ever seen the individuals before. As a seamstress who is well versed in historical attire, she could pinpoint the clothing down to the year. "It was definitely 1870s clothing, there was no doubt in my mind." The figures may have been solid and dark, but their clothing was distinct. Shortly after the figures were spotted, they were gone within a single blink. Shannon turned to Jake and asked in a surprised and incredulous tone, "Did you see that?" Jake nodded in amazement, unable to verbalize what he had just witnessed.

After two years of strange occurrences at the gallery, Shannon reached out to the Tri-City Ghost Hunters Society to do a paranormal investigation on November 13, 2009. Four female investigators were present that evening, as was Shannon. The team split up into groups of two and three. While three ladies were downstairs looking into the basement, Ellen Beauchamp and another female investigator were present upstairs. As they were sitting in the entrance conducting an electronic voice phenomena (EVP) session, which consists of attempting to capture voices unheard by human ears on a digital recorder, they noticed two Victorian figures pass by the window at about three o'clock in the morning. The man and woman were wearing darkened period clothing, and their features were nearly impossible to make out, although it could clearly be seen that the woman figure was holding a black parasol. As they crossed by the window, they were laughing and truly seemed to enjoy being in each other's company. They were heading north down Adams Street toward the back of the Bay City Post Office, and as they passed the doorway of the studio, they could no longer be seen or heard. They had entirely vanished. Ellen did not say anything to Shannon until much later, when she was telling her about the team's experiences at the gallery, and Shannon admitted to seeing the same exact people outside the window.

While reviewing the evidence from the investigation, an unrecognizable voice was captured; it sounded like a man with an English or Irish accent saying, "Ma'am, straight ahead." With all female investigators present that evening, hearing a man chime in on the recording was unnerving and alarming. None of the investigators present had an English or Irish accent either.

A month after the paranormal investigation, in December 2009, Justin and Shannon closed Belle Epoque's doors for the last time. Unfortunately, their

The area outside of the Belle Epoque Art Gallerie where shadowy Victorian figures have been reported during the wee hours of the morning. *Author photo*.

leasing contract was expiring, and due to legal issues with the condominium developer, the bank took back ownership of the portion of the building that was occupied by the gallery. It was far too expensive to buy the location back from the bank, so an executive decision was made to let their gallery go. The space sat vacant until 2013, when a clothing store moved in and made major changes to the décor, leaving Belle Epoque a memory of the past.

While it is puzzling who the Victorian-clad individuals are and why they remain attached to this portion of the Shearer Brothers Building, it has been speculated that these individuals are in mourning. During Queen Victoria's reign in the United Kingdom (1837–1901), black mourning dress became extremely popular among both the British and American peoples. On December 14, 1861, when Queen Victoria lost her husband, Prince Albert, she was so devastated by the loss that she wore mourning attire for the rest of her life. She was credited with setting the standard of that time for how to properly grieve. Whenever a sovereign or loved one passed away, it was a requirement to wear only black clothing for at least three months and in some cases almost three years. Mourning dress was offered to all social classes, but those who could not afford to completely revamp their wardrobes usually dyed their everyday clothing black. How much black clothing people wore depended on what stage of mourning they were in. Generally, someone who was in the early stages of mourning wore all black, while those who were in the later stages would wear hints of white and purple in addition to all black. The ghostly twosome had only ever been spotted in entirely black clothing. Today, the legend continues that if you are outside the Shearer Brothers Building on Adams Street during the wee hours of the morning, you may encounter the shadowed Victorians as well. Do not forget to pay them your respects.

6

GEAUX TO THE LIGHT

According to a Live Science poll, a whopping 71 percent of people in America have reported experiencing paranormal activity. Some of these people may never have another encounter in their lifetimes. However, for Justin and Shannon Rodriguez, this was not the case. When the Memorial Presbyterian Church on Lafayette Avenue was put up for sale in January 2016 due to diminishing membership, Justin believed it would be the perfect place to relocate his tattoo shop and preserve a valuable property within the city. For 123 years, this church had been serving the religious needs of the public, and with tasteful homage to its history, the church saw a major change of business. On May 13, 2016, Justin and Shannon purchased the building for $35,000. While this gem erected in 1870 was now in their possession, it did not come without surprises. It came with not only the Holy Spirit but also the resident ghost of a deceased pastor who served the church for over thirty years. This was the second haunted business location the Rodriguezes found themselves drawn to. For this paranormal-loving couple, it was no other than Shearer luck.

The Memorial Presbyterian Church was originally built as a large Sunday school in November 1871. Just two years later, the Sunday school was converted into a church as the Presbyterian faith expanded around the city and the need for more churches grew. Since the church's beginning, the congregation has prided itself on being like a family. There were craft festivals, potlucks and fundraisers, as well as an adult and children's choir that regularly performed concerts. A youth group was established and sponsored

This photograph was taken while Reverend Perry V. Jenner was the pastor of Memorial Presbyterian Church, circa late 1890s. *Courtesy of Jon Essex (former pastor of the church).*

by Earl and Opal Wahl. The children would be taken on adventures around the state and country, including visits to the Silver Springs State Park in Ocala, Florida, during the winter months. Among the parish, there was also a Mariner's Group for married couples to get to know one another and mingle, a men's club and various clubs for women.

In the 1940s and 1950s, the church was at the height of its popularity. There were 200 members on record at that time and 120 children attending the Sunday school. If visitors were to enter the church for service, they may not have been able to find seats. People had no choice but to stand if they wanted to be a part of the worship because the pews were packed. As the years went on, membership began to decrease little by little, until it seemed there was hardly any congregation left. By January 11, 2015, there were only a reported 32 members, and keeping the church open became a financial burden. While no one had been able to pinpoint a reason for this decline, the church had experienced hardship with getting new members to join in place of ones who had passed away. In recent years, the churches in the Bay City area have been affected by a drop in registered members. There had been speculation among remaining members that the church at 312 Lafayette Avenue was permanently closing, and members were devastated by the idea. For many, this place had been like a second home to them. A poll was held to decide whether to close the church once and for all. As reluctant as people were to have a hand in the church's demise, on November 16, 2015, there was a majority vote to shut down religious operations.

Due to a fascination with and love for religion, Shannon and Justin felt as though they had hit the jackpot when they stumbled across the advertisement that showcased this gorgeous church. "The possibilities when I saw the church seemed endless," Justin said. Voodoo Tattoo, which used to occupy 1010 Columbus Avenue, had always displayed the Rodriguezes faith in forms of statues, crosses and art pieces. After they purchased the church, the building underwent major renovations. Sometime between the 1960s and 1970s, the interior had been remodeled with yellow paneling, red carpet and industrial doors, while the exterior was painted an unattractive shade of white that had discolored over the years. One glance at the building and the new owners started planning for a much-needed transformation. However, there was one thing that remained the same. The fact that this was an ecclesiastical structure meant a lot to Justin and Shannon, and despite the building being totally stripped and renovated, they kept the altar perfectly intact. As a devout Catholic, Shannon has been collecting religious iconology since she was twelve years old and found this reformed church the

A service at the Memorial Presbyterian Church in the fall of 2010. *Courtesy of Heidi Prince.*

The beautiful stained-glass windows can still be viewed at the site today. *Courtesy of Heidi Prince.*

perfect place to display her collection. In addition to preserving the altar, the building's exterior and stained-glass windows were conserved as well. After a $150,000 renovation, Voodoo Tattoo, a great place to get inked, has become a religious museum of sorts as well.

As historic preservationists and part-time New Orleans residents, Justin and Shannon had their work cut out for them when they began restoring the church to its original grandeur with a Crescent City flair. They not only had paints hand mixed that represented the colors of the temples and parlors of the Voodoo religion that they had visited down South, but they also had glossy antique floor tiles shipped in from Europe. Every detail of their shop's past as a church and Big Easy theme was considered in the renovation process. The southern shade of haint blue graces the ceiling in order to ward off evil spirits, while an orangey-yellow hue attracts curious observers from the outside. Other various vibrant colors, including traditional Mardi Gras colors of green and purple, cover the walls. Surprisingly, the locals were exceedingly supportive of this change in business, and few individuals in the community, including followers of Leviticus, found the change to be blasphemous. Bay City officials were extremely supportive and happy that the building was being saved by such a respectful couple. When Voodoo Tattoo had its open house, other churches donated some of their religious iconology to Shannon's massive collection within the shop. To outsiders, the combination of what appears to be two drastically different religions may seem strange. However, to Shannon and Justin, the combination was a seamless integration.

Voodoo is arguably the most misunderstood religion practiced today. It was first introduced in the United States by way of enslaved West Africans who were transported to New Orleans, Louisiana. These individuals had merged their religious practices with Catholicism, and thus, the Voodoo religion was born. Voodoo practiced in the United States is also referred to as Voodoo-Catholicism. Voodoo believes in building a connection with ancestors, nature and spirits, despite its being portrayed in movies and media as dark and aggressive. Surprisingly, Voodoo dolls are more of a pop culture novelty item than an actual religious icon. Voodoo brought comfort to many during the slave revolt in 1791, when followers escaped Haiti and relocated to New Orleans. Many liberated people of color had adopted the practice of Voodoo and viewed it as culturally important. Voodoo is believed to help common physical and mental ailments such as depression, loneliness, sadness, hunger and sickness. In the 1800s, many of the most important spiritual and political influencers were Voodoo kings and queens. Those who practice Voodoo simply believe that God is not intervening in one's daily life, but that spirits are instead. Through dancing, music, chanting and snakes, one can contact the spirits much like prayer is believed by Christians to speak to God.

Despite the lack of wild dancing and snake handling, the church's long-dormant resident spirit has awakened since the renovations began. Reverend Henry Kreulen, who headed the church from 1917 to 1950, is still actively keeping up appearances. The Dutch minister Henrikus "Henry" Kreulen passed away on December 17, 1957, and was buried in Oakhill Cemetery in Grand Rapids, Michigan. However, he was extremely proud of the thirty-three years he had dedicated to being a religious leader at the Memorial Presbyterian Church and was adored by many attendees over the years. His leaving the church and his passing were both greatly upsetting to those who came to know and admire him. Shortly after acquiring the building, Voodoo's maintenance man, Greg, and piercer, Jake, would spend the night in the basement for weeks at a time, protecting the building, as there was no security system at that time. The men stayed in what used to be the classroom portion of the basement, which is sandwiched between former church offices and a commercial kitchen. While in the basement, they reported hearing movement upstairs, particularly on Saturday and Sunday mornings. There was a noted pattern to the footsteps as if someone was getting ready for weekend service. Paul Gomez, the shop's senior tattoo artist, who works in one of the back booths, is the opener and has encountered the patterned walking as well. Everyone who has heard the footsteps, including the owners, stated that the path of the footsteps never changes. Greg, Jake and Paul have also experienced lights being turned on and off despite knowing the state that the rooms were left in prior to leaving them. Once the security system was installed, the activity picked up. The owners disclosed that the paranormal occurrences happen at least once a week, sometimes more.

One late evening while the Rodriguezes were in bed sleeping, their phones went off, notifying them that someone was in the tattoo shop. They jolted awake at this news and immediately began searching for who was in the building and why. After reviewing the security camera footage, it was apparent that the building was void of any trespassers. Several days after the incident, it happened again. And again. And *again*. The fact that something out of the norm was happening at Voodoo became harder and harder to ignore. After hours of doing restorative woodwork inside the building, Shannon and Justin decided to take a quick break and sat down on the altar. As they looked ahead into the empty church absent of pews, they imagined

The altar, pictured here in the fall of 2010, is still intact to this day, despite major renovations. It has been witness to some ghostly happenings. *Courtesy of Heidi Prince.*

how their finished shop would look. Suddenly, a broom that was resting against the wall floated clear across the room and relocated to the wall on the other side of the building. Shannon and Justin eyed the transporting tool totally flabbergasted, yet excited. A haunting had been speculated, but to have their speculations solidified was incredible.

Justin first came face to face with the long-deceased Reverend Kreulen one day while doing woodwork in the church vestibule. As he was working, he caught the eye of an older man who was sitting in the room, watching him detail the wood. Justin described him as being a heavy-set man with a rotund belly who was wearing dress pants and a white shirt with a tie. The man also sported a pair of outdated glasses. Justin knew immediately who this man was, as he had seen photographs of Reverend Kruelen and this figure was an identical match. After the initial surprise of realizing he was not alone in the room, he continued to work, while the figure monitored his every move. Shannon caught two glimpses of the reverend as well, noting that he was still wearing his dress clothes at the time that she saw him. "The first time I saw him, he was as solid as any other person, but the second time I saw him he was kind of glimmery," she said.

Reverend Henry Kreulen at the dedication of the new Kilgen pipe organ, Sunday, January 4, 1948. *Courtesy of Heidi Prince.*

The Memorial Presbyterian Church was painted blue in the mid-1990s. *Courtesy of Heidi Prince.*

In 2018, the basement of Voodoo Tattoo had two more businesses move in: Justin's T-shirt shop Mete Vodou—French for "Voodoo Wear"—and Shannon's candle business, Dark Candles. Shannon purchased the candle company from her friend Helena, a Latin professor who originally ran it until she got tenure at Texas A&M University. Since then, Shannon has grown the business and sells candles all over the world. With three separate, remarkably successful businesses being run in the same facility, it is no doubt that a lot of time is spent in all areas of the building. While the paranormal activity has calmed since the renovations have been completed, the weekend footsteps continue, as do sightings of the passed reverend. "We've approached these renovations with total respect. I think he knows that and he's just looking out for his beloved church," Shannon said smiling. "I feel total comfort knowing that he is still here."

7
SPIRIT GUIDES AND POSITIVE VIBES

Charlie and Chocolate Factory, the children's novel by author Roald Dahl, is considered his most famous work, and the book has sold over twenty million copies worldwide since its publication in 1964. The story has since been featured in motion pictures, popular culture and referenced in nearly every candy shop around the world. Even though there are dark elements to Dahl's story about the eccentric chocolatier who runs and operates one of the most creative and mysterious chocolate factories of all time, the story fills the reader with wonder and "pure imagination." One step into Tummy Ache Candy Store at 1116 North Johnson Street, and it is like you have stepped into the book. Starr and Michael Henning, the shop's owners, have created their own candy wonderland right here in Bay City. Tummy Ache Candy Store is located a short distance away from the downtown area in the Johnson Street Business District, nestled between residences and other businesses. Here one can find not only dozens of nostalgic and homemade sweets but a positive presence that inhabits the shop as well.

The Johnson Street Business District spans from Center Avenue to Woodside Avenue. It is an endearing little district containing a variety of shops, including a high-end hair salon, an Irish pub, a pharmacy, a vegetable market and eatery, a liquor store, florists and a dry cleaner. The district had been serving small businesses like these for over a century. It was the perfect part of town to open a fun little candy store.

The building that now houses Tummy Ache Candy Store was built in 1920. Little is known about the origins of the building itself. Many people speculate it was used solely for businesses, but according to city directories, the earliest date of any business occupying the building was when Goodwill Cleaners operated there from 1965 to 1968. The property then remained vacant for several years until Lambert Printing purchased the building in 1975. After Lambert Printing moved out, the building stood vacant for around eight years prior to the Hennings buying it.

Starr had moved to Bay City as a young woman, and five years after marrying her husband in 1991, they decided to begin a new adventure together. Wanting to branch out from the traditional nine-to-five lifestyle and go a more unconventional route, they acquired an ice cream truck that they named "Starshine" and would drive around town selling sweets. They parked the truck at their home when it was not in use, but they desired to take their dreams to the next level. Upon spotting their perfect business location, the Hennings immediately fell in love with the building. Totally scared of losing this perfect and spacious establishment after seeing various guests venture in and out of the doors alongside the property's realtor, they jumped on the opportunity to buy the building right away. While away

The exterior of Tummy Ache Candy Store in the Johnson Street Business District. *Author photo.*

on a vacation in California, they signed the paperwork to seal the deal. In 2000, they purchased the property on North Johnson Street with the goal of opening a Mexican restaurant and were pleasantly excited that they now had the perfect location to park Starshine as well. Unfortunately, the money needed to open the restaurant just wasn't there, so the Hennings decided to take the earnings they had saved up from five years of selling sugary confections and create a vibrant sweet shop for children and adults alike. The artsy couple put their heads together and created the magical candy land you see today. The brightly colored building stands out among the neutral-colored businesses and homes in the district. From the moment you step inside, it's like stepping straight into a child's imagination. Elements inside the shop pay homage to Alice in Wonderland and Willy Wonka's candy factory. Strung-up lights and animatronics add to the magic, especially during children's birthday parties. This place is unlike any other candy store in town for several different reasons.

Working hard while creating their candy utopia, Michael was in the back of the building cutting into the cement with a jackhammer, while Starr was up front organizing the lumber and plywood for use in the store. She had neglected to remember that a log was behind her. Stepping back, she tripped and began falling while holding a sharp sheet of wood in her hands. As she fell to the ground, lumber came crashing down around her and on top of her. She screamed "Please help me!" at the top of her lungs, but Michael, still working with loud machinery, did not hear her cries for help. After the dust had settled from the fall, Starr sat up in a panic, wondering if she had broken any bones. But miraculously, she was fine. She did not even have so much as a scratch on her. Starr knew throughout her entire life that she had a spiritual gift but generally did not speak to others about it for fear of judgment. However, it was at that moment she felt as if a protective male presence was looking out for her and accepted her spiritual abilities. This incident would neither be the first nor the last incident encountering this helpful spirit.

The Henning's son, Sky, grew up in the shop and would often help his mom and dad out with business chores. Whenever he had a free moment, he would play in the back and explore, as little kids often do. One day as he was playing, he heard, "Sky! Come here, Sky!" Sky immediately ran to the front of the store to his mother. "Mom, was that you calling for me? Did you need my help?" "No honey, I wasn't calling for you." They both initially dismissed it as a misunderstanding and did not think much more of it. That was, until it began to happen all the time. Sky would regularly hear his name being called out, only to discover that his mom or dad was not calling him. Perhaps it was just the helpful fellow who had previously protected his mother also looking out for him. Over time, it had been discovered that this spirit was not only protective and caring but a prankster as well. One day the Hennings came in early to prepare for a birthday party, and Starr had come down ill with the flu. Michael and a family friend came in to help set up the party room, while Starr tended to other duties. While working, she had gotten the urge to use the restroom, and as she closed the door behind her, she felt someone tap her behind. She was bemused and unimpressed by the goofy incident. Whoever remains attached to the candy shop must have known, because that was the first and last time such an incident ever occurred there. However, one of Starr's employees shared a similar, embarrassing incident where she was using the shop's restroom during a birthday party and the door sprang open on her. Early on, the employees and owners would also encounter the music in the shop being either cranked up or turned off, which initially was very confusing to the staff until they became used to the recurring activity.

A loyal customer of Tummy Ache Candy Store who has chosen to remain anonymous had what she believes to be a paranormal encounter in the shop. Although her encounter was more of a blessing than a curse. She recalled visiting the store with her four-year-old daughter during the holiday season, and they were looking around at the different candies and décor when she realized she had misplaced two twenty-dollar bills she had been holding in her hand. Trying to remain calm so as not to alarm her young daughter, she silently and frantically searched the store hoping they would turn up. She was just about to break the news to her daughter that they were going to have to leave because she had no money to spend on treats, when a man's voice whispered loudly and clearly into her ear, "Check the Jolly Ranchers." The woman swung around, expecting to see an employee, but no man was to be found. After a few seconds of searching for the correct jar, she saw the Jolly Ranchers label and lifted the lid. Stuffed inside was her two bills. She did not remember opening any jars, let alone putting her money inside them, but she felt that whoever or whatever led her to the jar was keeping the money safe for her until she found it.

In 2017, Dr. Ray Clark of Nobody Believes Me Paranormal and Alan Tolf of PoppaNana Paranormal collaborated together on conducting a paranormal investigation of Tummy Ache Candy Store. Starr, born with the gift of being a sensitive, was also present during the investigation. When Starr began speaking to the male spirit she believed to be present in the building, the melmeter, which is a dual-purpose meter that measures both the electromagnetic field and temperature in the environment, began to spike. Prior to the investigation, the electricity in the building had been shut down as to not interfere with any of the meters being used. The investigators were using a 12-587 spirit box, and a female voice came through saying, "Help me. I'm out. Can you see me?" Suddenly, the name "Tessa" kept being repeated, despite the belief that only a male spirit was in the shop. Starr asked, "Is Tessa here now?" The investigators did not think too much of the name until a voice came through and said, "Don't worry Alan, find Tessa." To have one of the investigators called out by name piqued their interest. At that point, Starr invited Tessa to come over and sit by her, causing a paranormal whirlwind to occur. Various pieces of equipment began to react—even meters in other rooms were going off. As Starr continued speaking to the spirits and feeling their presences growing stronger and stronger, her name was finally whispered over the box. Although it remains a mystery who Tessa is or was, she remains connected to the building in a peaceful form.

Ghost stories are notorious for being dark and dreary, but the ghost stories surrounding this candy store are as light and bright as the shop itself. The owners, employees and customers have all agreed that the paranormal encounters have been mostly playful and positive. Starr believes that this positive energy has given the business a great base. "Every time another successful year of business passes, I am thankful to whoever is looking out for me. I feel supported in my business. The building has great vibes. The energy in here is inspiring." Starr is not wrong. One visit to this shop and you will feel the presence of positivity too. Not only will you experience the hospitality of the staff and some of the best homemade ice cream treats and hand-dipped chocolates in the city, but you may also encounter the shop's spirit guides who take care of staff and customers alike.

8

A Hair-Raising Experience

L egend has it that in the middle of the twentieth century, a prominent local entrepreneur reported to his workplace in the upper level of 919 Saginaw Street for the very last time. It was a day like any other, or so he thought. Coming into work, dressed in his finest suit, he looked forward to another day of profit and productivity. During this era, it was popular to use conveyor belt systems to move items from the street level up to the second-story level. As the owner was actively focused on getting his precious cargo to where it needed to be, he was not paying attention. While on the second story intercepting inventory, he misjudged the distance of the ledge leading outdoors, overstepped and fell to the ground below, ultimately resulting in his untimely death. As employees stood in horror at what they had just witnessed, with their boss's blood painted on the concrete below, it was clear that this tragedy would not be forgotten and would forever live in the minds of those who witnessed it. That day, the energy of the building changed. Staff no longer felt comfortable entering the upper level, and to this very day, the staff and students of Bayshire Beauty Academy still feel that same energy lingering. It has resulted in some terrifying encounters over the years.

The building that now serves as the Bayshire Beauty Academy is divided by two separate addresses. The front entrance and cosmetology booths occupying the left-hand portion of the building make up 917 Saginaw Street, while the admissions office, massage therapy classrooms and second story on the right side make up 919 Saginaw Street. The use of 917 dates

Bayshire Beauty Academy as it looks in current times. *Author photo*.

back to the year 1885 when the City Mission provided aid to the homeless. In 1893, the City Mission became the Ellsworth Commission House and was still assisting those in poverty until 1901. Presley and Layer, an agricultural company, took over 917 when the Ellsworth Commission House moved out and remained in business until 1948, when James Dean Agricultural Imports moved in and stayed in business for a total of two years. This portion of the building then operated as the Northern Supply Company's Electrical Department until the company began selling auto parts and did so up until the beauty college was established. Initially used as a blacksmith shop, 919 Saginaw Street was established around 1900. In 1920, this part of the building began featuring different auto sale companies for a total of fifty-two years. Most notably, in 1935, the upstairs was used as the first Model T showroom in downtown Bay City, when the building was under management by Bayford Company Auto, Ford Sales and Service. It still houses the oldest car elevator of any business in the area. This popular location, in the heart of downtown Bay City, supported several businesses since the automotive companies closed their doors.

The birth of Bayshire all began when James "Jim" Goodrow Sr. decided he was ready for a much-needed change in his life. He had been in the parking lot business for several years and had owned a lot in Saginaw. While working one day, he met Howard Schmidt, a licensed barber who began to regularly use his parking lot. After doing some research of his own about the cosmetology industry, Jim Sr. decided to give this new career choice a shot. After obtaining his cosmetology license, he opened his first salon with his wife, Cherie Nan Goodrow (formerly Wolcott), called the Coif Salon on 2620 Center Avenue in April 1961. While looking for someone to manage the salon, he originally thought about offering the job to one of his instructors. However, after speaking with Schmidt regarding his career background, Jim Sr. found him to be much better suited for the position. Schmidt decided to accept the management position at the Coif. With Howard being one of the best barbers in the Tri-Cities, it was a no brainer that he was going to excel in this new role. Jim made a gentleman's agreement with Howard that if the salon succeeded, he would sell Howard a half interest in the salon, making him a co-owner. According to Jim's son, James Forest, during the 1960s, Bay City's cosmetology school was located beside where the Alice and Jack Wirt Library sits today on the corner of Adams Street and Center Avenue and directly across from the old JC Penney, which currently houses the City Market. The Bay City Beauty College was established in 1928, the same year that Jim Sr. was born, and it was a great place to learn the trade of being a hairdresser.

The fact that the Bay City Beauty College was established in 1928 makes perfect sense. It was the part of that decade when women were embracing more androgynous fashions and liberating themselves with short haircuts and hairdos that gave one the appearance of chopped locks. The most notable styles included bobs and finger waves. On May 1, 1920, the *Saturday Evening Post* published an article by journalist F. Scott Fitzgerald titled "Bernice Bobs Her Hair." The piece tells the tale of a naïve and socially awkward young woman who is fooled into getting her hair chopped off by a barber, much to the amusement of her jokester cousin. The cut results in her family disowning her and boys no longer being interested in her. The haircut became a symbol of dishonor and shame for her family. It sounds ridiculous now, but that's how greatly society prioritized women's long hair in the beginning of the twentieth century. Long hair was synonymous with great beauty and femininity. Of course, as the years went on, women began to rebel by cutting off their lengthy tresses. Many hairdressers would refuse to do business with these women, as they either did not want to be a part of something so controversial or simply had no idea how to cut hair so short. Women would leave salons and march straight into a barbershop requesting the short do inspired by Irene Castle, a trendsetting ballroom dancer from 1915. Barbers were more than happy to oblige. These rebellious and newly liberated young women who rocked their short dos were labeled "flappers." The idea of a woman's hair being her "crowning glory" was drastically changing. By 1925, the beauty industry had accepted bobs and even made claims that the style did wonders for business. Various styles of bobs became widely accepted, resulting in a mass need for hairdressing services across the United States. As the demand for more hair services grew, so did the industry. On September 1, 1937, the Board of Barbering, Cosmetology and Esthetics was established, and licensure was introduced.

Jim Goodrow Sr. was known for his infectious smile and friendly demeanor. *Courtesy of Jenae Prell, Bayshire Beauty Academy.*

After realizing how much of a passion he had for hairdressing, Jim Goodrow Sr. developed a desire to not only manage a salon but also teach the trade to others who had a love for it. Jim Sr. and Howard decided to branch out and purchase the Bay City Beauty College shortly after the establishment of the salon. Their purchase of the female-owned-and-operated beauty college landed them the prestigious title of "pioneers of gender equality" in the field of cosmetology, allowing other men to build careers traditionally for women. The two men named their newly purchased property Howard's Beauty Academy. After spending about five years on Center Avenue and Adams Street, Jim Sr. and Howard decided that a property with ground-level accessibility would better serve the public, including the elderly and differently abled individuals. In 1968, the two men purchased and relocated the beauty school to the location on 917 Saginaw Street, which was a vacant building at the time. Within thirty days of purchasing the property, the two men completely gutted and renovated the interior. What was the shell of a building was now a modern, inclusive and updated beauty school.

Cherie Goodrow, of English descent, inspired her husband to perfectly rename his brand-new school. In England, a county is called a shire. Because of the location of the school being in Bay County, Michigan, the name

Bayshire referred to the beauty academy of Bay County and thus, the name Bayshire Beauty Academy was created. Through genealogical research, it has been discovered that Cherie is actually a direct descendent of one of King Arthur's Knights of the Round Table, as well as Oliver Wolcott Sr., a brigadier general in the Continental army and the nineteenth governor of the state of Connecticut. This creative and appropriate name for the school is an accurate representation of its location and brought a little bit of Cherie's heritage a little closer to home. With the success of the new school, Jim Sr. began to focus all his efforts on instructing, and Howard took over the salon, renaming it Mr. Howard's Coif Salon. Jim Sr. became well known throughout the cosmetology community for being a passionate and hardworking individual and for his innovative ideas, inspiration and kindness he showed everyone he crossed paths with. Due to the growth and popularity of his beauty school and groundbreaking lesson plans, he became a revered icon throughout the state of Michigan. He was so determined to see his students succeed, he even assisted them with opening their own salons. After a lifetime of raising two children, his son, James Forest, and daughter Kathy Troup (Grundling), and working many long hours on his journey to success, Jim Sr. began dreaming of his retirement and who would take over his thriving business. After much thought and consideration, he called his son, who was living in Atlanta and working in Marietta, Georgia, at the time.

Never in a million years did James Forest ever think he would be owning and operating a beauty school. He was working on the Dobbins Air Reserve Base at one of the divisions of the Lockheed Martin Corporation as a customer support specialist. Working for the largest defense contractor in the United States, he was well versed in his knowledge of airplanes, submarine components, security and secret weapons, but hairstyling was not his expertise. When his father called and explained that he was ready to retire and offered up his business to his son, it was an offer James Forest just could not refuse. James Forest decided to move back to Bay City, Michigan, and with the help of his sister, Kathy, was able to make advancements in the operation of the school. In the 1980s, James Forest fell in love with a woman named Lisa who had attended the same elementary school and grew up in the same neighborhood. Lisa, coincidentally, decided she wanted to become licensed in the cosmetology field. While James Forest had no intentions of working among a bunch of aspiring hairdressers and cosmetology instructors, he seemed to be surrounded with those who had a passion for it, and over time, he grew to appreciate it too. In order to become the new

When getting ready to retire, Jim Goodrow Sr. called on family to take over his beloved business. *Courtesy of Jenae Prell, Bayshire Beauty Academy.*

beauty school owner, James Forest obtained his Cosmetology License and Limited Cosmetology Instructor License. Shortly thereafter, Lisa completed her licensure examinations and joined Bayshire in the 1990s. For decades, many businesses, students, faculty and clients have passed through Bayshire's doors, but not all of them have moved on.

For many years, there have been reports of eerie presences and creepy figures lurking throughout the school. One such figure left a student so terrified she was frozen in her tracks, unable to speak as it peered back at her from a dimly lit hallway. Nearing the hallway to the Fourth Street entrance, a cosmetology student saw a flicker in the distance. She curiously walked closer only to discover she was no longer alone and whatever was there could not possibly be human. She described the figure as resembling a demonic dog man. It stood upright like a human with its looming height but appeared big and bulky, with fur and razor-sharp claws. Its eyes were glowing like the dying embers in a fireplace at the end of the darkened corridor. Small orange glints could be seen blinking as the figure hungrily eyed the student. When she mustered up enough courage to turn and run, she refused to ever set foot in that hallway again. Of course, other students and staff thought she was crazy once she told them about her encounter. A vicious dog man roaming Bayshire? Claims of Bayshire being haunted? Surely this student was losing her mind, and for a long time, everyone all thought so, until they began having encounters of their own. Marilyn Eddy, the massage therapy school founder, began having so many spine-tingling experiences that she decided to bring it to the attention of James Forest. As she was a well-respected instructor and colleague, people began taking the claims of paranormal activity more seriously. Of course, not everyone saw the feared animalistic creature, but different men. Men that looked off. Men that were not of this period. The most reported figure in the school has been referred to as "Eric." Every time he has been seen, he is wearing an old denim mechanics outfit, which consists of dark indigo bib overalls with rolled up pantlegs.

On Wednesday, November 20, 2019, at about 2:30 in the afternoon, Hunter Roebuck, a part-time massage student, was staying after school hours to work on his anatomy coloring book. The only people present in this portion of the building besides Hunter were the massage instructor and two full-time students, as everyone else had gone home for the day. The full-time students had agreed to do a relaxation massage on each other with incorporated myofascial techniques. The instructor invited Hunter to observe the massage session, but he opted to continue working on his schoolwork. As he was sitting at his desk labeling the bones of the feet in his coloring book, he noticed movement in his peripheral vision. Based on the classroom seating arrangement, Hunter thought he knew the identity of his classmate. At first, he did not pay her any mind because he figured it was one of the full-time students returning to her desk to get something. Soon the figure was directly in front of him, and he briefly glanced up, catching a glimpse of dark denim overalls, but he did not look up enough to see a face. Once again, he blew it off as nothing and went back to his work. Although massage students are required to wear scrubs at the school, he had figured this student had changed into something more comfortable before heading home. The figure continued rummaging through belongings at the desk opposite Hunter for several minutes. As soon as Hunter was finished labeling the feet bones in his book, he lifted his head and said, "Hey, sorry I was working on my coloring book. What are you searching for?" only to discover that no one was there. Hunter sat in stunned silence until the instructor entered the room and laughed at the sight of him. "You look like you've just seen a ghost," she remarked. "Take a break from your book and come join us in the massage room. I want to show you skin rolling and transverse friction massage." As Hunter got up and followed the teacher into the massage room, his eyes almost fell out as the student he believed to be in the room with him just moments earlier was undressed under the sheet on the massage table! Two weeks later, when a door banged shut, someone jokingly said, "Oh, that's just Eric!" At that point, Hunter learned the story of the man in the denim overalls that staff and students have been reporting for years. He has been known to slam doors, turn lights on and off and appear at the most inconvenient of times, especially in the evening when the school is being locked up for the night, causing stress to staff who believe everyone is not out of the building. Based on the style and clothing, Eric is believed to have been a mechanic in 1935 for the Ford dealership that occupied the building. While there are no reports of a mechanic dying on the property during this time, this entity obviously is passionate about still calling this building his home away from home.

A group of Bayshire staff and students did a paranormal investigation one evening on the second level of 919 Saginaw Street with the hopes of contacting the deceased entrepreneur that fell to his death decades before. While investigating, a series of pictures was taken in an attempt to capture any spirits present. Later, while going through the photographs, one of the staff noticed that a few of the photos included light anomalies. However, one photograph had a grainy, yet distinguishable figure of an elegantly dressed man. It appeared from the photograph that this figure was garbed in a top hat and topcoat, displayed a dark dapper mustache and had mangled limbs. Was the group successful in capturing a photograph of the late businessman, or was someone else horribly disfigured and killed in an earlier workplace death? We may never know.

The history of Bayshire's ghosts remains a mystery to this day. So far, three entities have made their presences known, but could there be more? The building has a long and varied history, much like its current ghostly inhabitants. Beginning as a soup kitchen for the poor, witnessing the end of the lumbering era and the emergence of the automotive industry and now being utilized as a prominent beauty school in a modern midwestern city, Bayshire may have skeletons in its closet. Schedule a shampoo and blowout sometime—your hair may just rise on its own.

9

SCANDAL, SPOOKS AND SLAUGHTER

By the early 1900s, Bay City was undergoing a drastic change. Police were cracking down on the crime with the goal that a more wholesome crowd would become drawn to the area. Of course, those who had profited off their corrupt ways during the peak of the lumbering area just learned how to disguise their work in such a way to make it appear somewhat respectable. In 1908, the Bijou Theatre was built at 913 Washington Avenue, just blocks away from the notorious Water Street. The theater, originally intended to be used as a vaudeville and burlesque house, was also being utilized as a brothel behind the scenes. In 1908, it was much easier for society to engage in sexual acts for money without fear of dire consequences. Until the federal government passed the Mann Act of 1910, there was no legislation controlling prostitution, and these lewd acts were generating large amounts of revenue for the theater. By 1915, almost all fifty states had banned what many refer to as "the oldest profession," and prostitution had been criminalized in every state with the hopes of preventing sex trafficking. Unfortunately, if caught by law enforcement, the working girls were the first to be jailed, but the buyers were not penalized. Although the Edwardian era was a notably modest time in American history, racy burlesque shows quickly skyrocketed in popularity, especially among curious and lustful members of society. In addition to a well-rounded show, featuring everything from comedy skits to musical performances, patrons were also treated to an on-stage striptease by women in glittering costumes, feathers and bedazzled lingerie without

A postcard of the Bijou Theatre in Bay City, circa 1908. *Courtesy of Paul Phillips, State Theatre.*

tights. Scandalous shows were no doubt the talk of the community, but throughout its varied history, the theater gained even more notoriety when a phantom was spotted throughout the building.

By the 1920s, the theater's name was changed to the Orpheum, and it was featuring risqué movies, in addition to still operating as a house of burlesque. For the next seven years, the theater was immersed in a sexual whirlwind. By the Roaring Twenties, the burlesque community had fully embraced and flaunted the sleazy and raunchy aspects of this form of entertainment. As film began to gain more popularity across the states, theater owners began advertising bawdy adult entertainment in a desperate means to keep their businesses open. Stripping catapulted to the forefront of burlesque shows, and it became an expectation for dancers to undress down to flimsy G-strings and pasties, much to the dismay of law enforcement. Any attempts to undress further would have resulted in being arrested for indecent exposure. However, the pornographic films previewed at the theater were even more intense in terms of sexual content, and self-serving individuals from all over the state came to watch these controversial motion pictures. These massive crowds of forlorn men that fled to the Orpheum Theatre to view the sexually explicit shows and films kept the theater running before, during and after the Great Depression. As time went on, the shock value began to wear off, and the film industry began to take over many theaters that featured live performances, including the Orpheum Theatre. In 1930, the theater's name was changed once again to the Bay Theatre. It underwent renovations that turned it into a Mayan temple, per the design of C. Howard Crane, an architect who also designed two identical Fox theaters, one in Detroit, Michigan, and one in St. Louis, Missouri.

During the wartime 1940s, theaters across the United States were being swarmed with business, and the Bay Theatre was no exception. At this time in history, movies and radio were the most common forms of entertainment among the working class, and any opportunity to see a show was enthusiastically taken. Floyd Ackerman, who managed both the Bay and the Regent Theatres in Bay City, was considered a local celebrity. Wearing his finest tuxedo and kindest smile, he would graciously greet guests of the theater, always making them feel warmly welcomed. He was adored by all his staff and was extremely proud of his role as manager. Never one to abuse his position of power, he was a pleasure to work for and be around. However, one theatergoer aimed to put on an act that would affect Ackerman and his supporters forever.

It was the night of Sunday, December 5, 1943. A movie had just finished at the Bay Theatre, and the audience members were making their way to the exit. Twenty-two-year-old Korean murderer Yuen "Johnny" Woos was among the crowd. He had previously taken the life of a Chinese man from Detroit he believed had abused his mother and had served a two-year sentence in the Ionia youth prison for manslaughter. Once he was released from prison, Woos relocated to Bay City. The city was heavily populated by immigrants of French Canadian, German and Polish descent, and with Woos being of Asian descent, he was easily identifiable. Woos exited from his balcony seat cleverly disguised by a convincing scar on his cheek created by stage makeup. As the theater cleared out, Ackerman was going about his usual managerial duties and headed to a bank on Fifth Street to deposit $1,700 in weekend receipts. Woos spotted Ackerman leaving the building and stealthily made his way to the post office across the street, where he could further watch Ackerman's actions. Woos quietly trailed behind Ackerman to the People's Commercial Bank, south on Washington Avenue, making sure not to make a sound or draw any attention to himself. When Ackerman finally made his way to the deposit box, he prepared his documents, opened the box up and was just about to insert them when he was startled by the unsettling demands of a madman. As Ackerman turned to face Woos, the color drained from his face when he saw that Woos had a gun pointed directly at him. "Stick 'em up!" Woos shouted angrily. Ackerman was partially in disbelief that such a thing was happening to him, but terror at the idea of losing his life began to rip through every fiber of his being. Ackerman, surging with adrenaline, turned to Woos and yelled loudly into the night, "You've got to be kidding!" Woos, alarmed by Ackerman's shouting, pulled the trigger of his gun twice, causing Ackerman to fall to the ground in a bloodied daze. Twelve individuals, including an officer of the law, saw the exchange take place. As people rushed to Ackerman's aid, Woos fled the scene. Ackerman was rushed to Mercy Hospital, and although he received prompt medical care for his gunshot wounds, he lost the fight for his life on the hospital bed. The citizens of Bay City and frequent visitors of the Bay Theatre were devastated by the news. The unjust murder of this kindhearted man had left a permanent stain on Bay City's theater community.

For a month, Woos evaded capture by law enforcement for killing Ackerman. That was until John Olepa, an undercover detective for the Michigan State Police, caught him in a gambling house on Washington Avenue. Once he was in custody, officers went to his boardinghouse room and decided to search for evidence. Upon tearing up the floorboards, they located a hidden sum of approximately $1,000, which led to Woos's arrest. In court, the judge assumed Woos's guilt and asked him why he committed the murder. In a moment of total transparency, Woos admitted to the crime and was sentenced to twenty-four years in prison. While in prison, Woos obtained access to legal books, studied them and filed multiple appeals. The appeals board continued to deny his requests for freedom. During this time, Woos acted as his own lawyer representing himself.

March 18, 1963, was a turning point for Woos that he was not even aware of. Supreme Court decision *Gideon v. Wainwright* allowed for defendants facing criminal charges the right to an attorney, whether they could afford them or not. Clarence Gideon committed a felony in Panama City, Florida, and the trial judge denied Gideon's request for the court to provide him an attorney because he did not have the means to afford one. Gideon's conviction was overruled, and he was able to have a second trial with an attorney present and acquitted of the original crime. Originally, this law was provided to people accused of felonies or greater crimes. Since then, this law has been extended to cover misdemeanor and juvenile crimes as well.

Eugene Penzien and David Skinner, two local attorneys, filed an appeal on behalf of Woos in front of a Pontiac jury, located eighty-seven miles south of Bay City, where the crime occurred. In the trial, the police used racist remarks when speaking to Woos, and another man sporting a scar along his cheek bone had been arrested. These behaviors and the fact that Woos was not allowed a public defender caused reasonable doubt among the second jury. Woos was released from prison in 1967 and relocated to Detroit, where he lived for an additional thirty-two years, eventually passing away in 1999. Woos occasionally came back to Bay City to reward those who had shown him kindness when he otherwise was met with hostility for his crimes and race. While Woos was able to leave prison and live out the remainder of his life as a free man, Floyd Ackerman's spirit remains trapped inside the theater to this day, searching for retribution. A balcony seat is dedicated in Ackerman's honor.

Despite the loss of Ackermann, "the show must go on," and it most certainly did. In the 1950s, the theater was beginning to show signs of deterioration, and Butterfield Theatres Incorporated purchased the building with the intent to give it a more modernized appearance. The entire Mayan temple theme was disguised, and the entirety of the interior of the building was painted a drab shade of brown. The marquee was also updated to look like those of other popular theaters around the country, stripping the building of its character. During this era, the theater underwent one last name change as well and was renamed State Theatre.

In the 1990s, owner Tim O'Brien attempted to keep the spirit of the theatre alive by showing movies for only one dollar, hoping to keep an interest in the local theater and open it up to families who couldn't afford visiting pricier venues. Unfortunately, due to the extensive number of repairs needing to be done, the low cost of admission was simply not enough to keep the theater in business. Other theaters in the area began to shift to a multiplex style. They were being constructed in both malls and freestanding locations. The State Theatre fell victim to neglect, and in 1999, it was closed to the public with no plans to reopen. After a year of the theater sitting vacant, the city had grown tired of seeing the empty building sitting in the middle of the downtown area and decided to demolish it and turn the ground beneath it into a parking lot. However, a group of people with a great appreciation for the State Theatre decided to protest demolition in order to preserve one of the oldest theaters in Bay City. These individuals banded together to create a

The theater, pictured here about 1970, was once stripped of its Mayan temple theme. *Courtesy of Paul Phillips, State Theatre.*

preservation society, Friends of the State Theatre, which eventually became a registered nonprofit. With this society, not only was the theater saved, but its history was honored as well. The group was brave enough to take on the task of restoring the Mayan temple theme, which took a total of five years. They were also able to expand the stage for a multitude of events, in addition to showing movies; re-create and incorporate the theater's original carpeting and paint colors into the décor; update their technology and lighting for shows; and reinstate a modernized digital version of the original marquee. To this day, the group remains committed to a never-ending effort of improving this historic theater and features everything from concerts of touring popular musical artists, lectures, weddings, town hall meetings, church services, comedy shows, movies and theatrical performances. For one current employee, these events have brought her job security and paranormal phenomena as well.

Brenda Baker, the current director of customer service, is not only savvy in her people skills but also a true wizard at selling tickets, supervising volunteers and managing the theater's social media accounts. After having paranormal encounters in her personal life, she turned to paranormal television shows to gain a better understanding about life after death. While seeking employment within the historic State Theatre, she was curious if any spectral beings roamed its halls. She remembered her job interview in the late summer of 2015 as if it were yesterday. Brenda made her way into the theater to meet with Michael Bacigalupo, chief operating officer, and Paul Phillips, director of operations. As Brenda sat down for her interview, she suspiciously eyed the room. "Could this place, by chance, be haunted?" Michael shot a quick glance at Paul and then turned back to Brenda with a gentle smirk. "There have been some things, but you'll be okay, Brenda. I promise." Brenda eyed the two men cautiously, using her eyes once more to scan the entirety of the room around her. "I just want to know what I am getting myself into," she said. Soon enough, Brenda would find out the truth all on her own.

Brenda's interview was a smashing success, and she was hired in August. She worked long hours at the theater to ensure everything ran smoothly but didn't have any paranormal encounters there until December 2015. With only a staff of three people, Brenda often works late nights, sometimes alone. It was a blistering cold winter day. Brenda had worked all morning and into the evening preparing for the Bijou orchestra to come and perform at the theater. At about six o'clock in the evening, as she walked through the aisle 2 door into the auditorium, she heard the distinct sound of a crowd of people laughing and mingling behind her in the lobby. She immediately darted out into the lobby to find the source of the commotion, but no one was in the building except for her. From that moment forward, whenever Brenda's shift comes to an end and she exits throughout the back door of the theater, she makes sure to turn on the theater lights as she makes her way out. She has even admitted to occasionally running to the parking lot through the theater in order to avoid any encounter with the dead. There is truly nothing more unsettling than being in pitch darkness with a group of people surrounding you that are not even alive.

A young woman who had worked in the box office prior to Brenda came back one night to volunteer for an event. While Brenda worked alongside the former employee, she learned the grim story of Floyd Ackerman's murder and the many ghost stories that have accompanied it over the years. The young woman told Brenda of one unexplainable incident that occurred while she was working at the ticket booth. As the woman was going about her morning duties, she heard someone in the theater with her and spotted a shadow figure out of the corner of her eye. She assumed nothing of it, as she just believed that Paul had entered the back door of the theater and was passing through the concession lobby. After completing the project that she was working on just minutes later, she entered the concession area to say good morning to Paul but could no longer hear anyone else in the building. After a thorough check of the upper and lower levels and repeated efforts of calling out to him, she had no luck locating anyone and went back to the ticket booth to resume her job. After confirming with Paul that he was not at the theater during that time, she realized she was no longer in the company of the living.

Paul Phillips, one of the employees with the highest seniority at the theater, was working at the soundboard, installing the new sound system in the auditorium, when he had heard the basement door near the aisle 2 entrance open. As soon as he stopped what he was doing to listen, the door slammed shut and latched. He was completely alone in the building. Although the incident did not really spook Phillips, it had certainly validated Brenda's previous experience. This incident involving the basement has been one of many. Over the years, volunteers, media personnel, special guests, visitors and staff have reported seeing the ghost of Ackerman meandering around the basement, as well as in the auditorium, especially up in the balcony. His slender, well-dressed figure pops up at the most random times. One minute you will be alone, rummaging through supplies or sitting down watching a performance, then suddenly he is there in the room with you, standing or sitting directly next to you, curious about what you're doing in his treasured theater and watching closely for a glimpse of Woos. Brenda, intrigued by the theater's dark past, enjoys hearing Paul's stories. While her morbid curiosity about Ackerman certainly keeps her job anything but boring, it has also had an affect on her work. She said,

> When you enter the auditorium, on the left-hand side of the room, there is a door hidden behind a curtain located nearby the emergency exit. Beyond that door, you enter a small hallway that leads to the back alley, but on the way to the alley there is another door that then descends into a storage area. We used to keep our merchandise down there. I do not like going down there unless I absolutely have to. It's so creepy. It freaks me out too much.

However, for Brenda and the other members on staff, the eerie atmosphere is just another day in the life of a State Theatre employee. It is true what they say—truth is, indeed, stranger than fiction.

Bay City native Carrie Smith attended State Theatre's spring break movie week in March 2017 with her sister, Brittany. During the movie, she realized that she needed to use the restroom, so she quietly snuck out of the auditorium to not disturb other viewers. As she made her way into the vacant bathroom, she did a makeup and clothing check in the mirror and entered a stall to do her business. Seconds after she locked the door and sat down, she heard what sounded like someone at the sink, washing their hands. Not thinking anything of it, as it is a public restroom, she had finished up and was just about to stand up when she noticed a pair of shiny black men's shoes facing her from beneath the stall door, peeking out from underneath a pair of black dress pants. "Excuse me," she said. "Someone is in here." The shoes remained facing her, in a fixed position, without so much as a single tap. "I am in here!" she said a little more assertively, becoming frustrated that the individual would not back away from the door. Suddenly, the feet stepped closer, now just inches away from Carrie's feet inside the stall with her. In a moment of panic, she slammed the inside of the stall door with both of her hands. "Back up! I am in here! What the hell is your problem?" The feet took a step back and suddenly it sounded as if fingernails were being dragged slowly across the door. Extremely disturbed at this point, Carrie tried to catch a glimpse of the individual doing this but could not see anything other than the feet and legs in the space beneath the door. With her growing discomfort, she quietly yanked her pants up and slowly reached for the lock when she saw the glimpse of a lengthy finger tracing the edge of the door nearby the lock. She flew back in surprise and became angry. "That's it! I have had enough! How dare you come into this restroom and harass someone in a stall. Get a life!" Just as Carrie shouted the last word, she used all her weight to fling the door open with as much force as she could muster, hoping to alarm whoever was on the other side. But surprisingly, when she pushed the door open, no one was there. She flung the door open to every stall and bolted out into the second-floor hallway in a desperate attempt to find the person responsible for taunting her in the bathroom. Carrie raced back to her seat and pulled Brittany aside. "Someone was in the bathroom with me, scratching on the stall door!" Brittany turned to her, giggling. "Carrie, it was probably just a kid. Relax." "It was not a kid! I saw the shoes and pants. They definitely belonged to a grown man!" Brittany burst out laughing loudly and jokingly rolled her eyes. "Carrie, I highly doubt a man would've followed you into the bathroom simply to harass you. Come on, girl." "Whatever," Carrie shot back, feeling annoyed. At the end of the movie, Brittany needed to use the bathroom, but Carrie refused to go with her, still feeling irritated by not being believed, and nervous to have another uncomfortable experience. "I'm going to have a smoke. I'll just wait outside for you."

A few ladies were in line with their children to use the restroom before Brittany, so she had to wait until the line dissipated. Finally, a stall became available, and although she doubted Carrie's experience, she took comfort in the fact that others were in the restroom with her. While in the bathroom, Brittany got a heated text from her boyfriend and became distracted. As she quickly typed messages back and forth, she didn't realize that the bathroom had cleared out around her. She exited the stall and, after washing her hands, leaned in closer to the mirror to inspect a blemish forming on her cheek. As she was focused on picking at it, she saw something in the mirror's reflection move behind her in the bathroom. As she brought her eyes upward over her left shoulder, she saw a well-dressed gentleman standing behind her. She jumped at the sight and fired back with an attitude, "You do realize that this is the women's bathroom, right?" Before Brittany could turn around and say another word, the figure behind her evaporated. Brittany caught her terrified reflection in the mirror, sprinted down the staircase to the first level and ran out the main doors to meet up with Carrie. "What took you so long? I was about to head home without you." Brittany burst into tears at the shock of what she had just witnessed. "Oh come on, I wasn't really going to head home without you. I was just kidding, Brittany!" Carrie said consoling her sister. Brittany looked at Carrie straight on, chewing her cheeks and lips anxiously. "I saw him. I saw the man. I believe you, and I'm sorry that I initially did not." As the two sisters walked to the car, Brittany told Carrie the whole story from start to finish. After doing some research, both ladies believed that they had encountered Ackerman in the bathroom that day. "The State Theatre can now add the women's bathroom to their list of paranormal hotspots," Brittany said. "I totally thought he was alive, just like we are, until I literally saw him vanish. I am at a loss for words of what I have witnessed. This is truly one of the strangest things I have ever had happen in my life."

As the sun sets and casts shadows on Bay City's State Theatre, one cannot help but be saddened and angered by the unjust killing by such a cold-blooded murderer all these years later. Floyd Ackerman represents our family, friends and neighbors. He represents every compassionate man and woman you get used to seeing around town. He was a beautiful soul taken from the world far too soon, now trapped in a realm that humanity has yet to fully understand. His loss was painful not only because he was good-natured and well-known but also because what happened to him could easily happen

Visit the State Theatre for a performance, and you just may come face to face with resident ghost, Floyd Ackerman. *Author photo.*

to any of us. We could find ourselves in the wrong place at the wrong time and fall victim to the same fate. While it is true that some of his appearances have left people terror-stricken, we must remember that he was once a living, breathing person. Maybe he was a prankster in life, or perhaps he is just trying to get someone's attention in order to get the help he so desperately seeks. No matter the approach he takes, one thing is for sure—his loyalty to the State Theatre is undeniable and everlasting.

CONCLUSION

Whether or not you are a believer in the afterlife, there is no disputing that hauntings have been reported since the earliest days of civilization on every continent and in every country, state, province, city, town and village across the entire world. Dating back to the first century AD, Pliny the Younger, a famous author and politician, was one of the first individuals to document the ghost sightings that he encountered at his home in Athens, Greece. He described the ghost in his house as having long facial hair and bound by chains that rattled with every step. This type of ghost has made its way into modern popular culture and was the inspiration behind Gus, one of the Hitchhiking Ghosts in Disney's Haunted Mansion. The term *poltergeist*, German for "noisy ghost," caught attention in AD 856, hundreds of years after Pliny the Younger detailed his own personal paranormal experience. According to historical research, a spirit was reported to have been causing a ruckus at a country homestead in Germany, hurling stones at the inhabitants of the home and even setting the farmhouse ablaze. Anne Boleyn, who reigned as England's queen from 1533 to 1536, was ordered to be decapitated by her own husband, King Henry VIII, at the Tower of London. She had many charges against her, including engaging in witchcraft, participating in incest, committing treason against her country and being an adulterer. Over the years, thousands have reported seeing her beheaded ghost with her head held firmly in the crook of her arm at many different locations, such as the Tower of London, Hever Castle, Hampton Court Palace and Windsor Castle, among others.

Ghosts of American leaders, such as Benjamin Franklin, Abraham Lincoln and Franklin D. Roosevelt have had reported sightings time and time again. Lincoln, murdered by John Wilkes Booth on April 14, 1865, by a bullet to the head, is the most reported spirit of all deceased political figures in America. He has been spotted at Ford's Theatre in Washington, D.C., as well as the White House, still carrying on with his presidential duties. According to a 2017 survey by Chapman University, three-fourths of Americans admitted to believing in some aspect of the paranormal, whether that be the existence of ghosts, aliens, telepathy, Bigfoot or otherwise. While it was difficult to locate studies about paranormal beliefs around the world, in addition to American studies, I was able to locate paranormal belief statistics in Asia. Some 90 percent of people in Japan and Taiwan have reported seeing ghosts, and that number is assumed to be just as high in China, Vietnam, and Korea. These countries embrace the paranormal far more than Western culture, although we are getting there. While there are some fantastic paranormal conventions in the United States, and Halloween is a significant cultural holiday in America, Asian countries observe a Ghost Month, which takes place in the seventh lunar month. The Hungry Ghost Festival, considered one of the scariest times of the year, takes place on the fifteenth day of the month and provides a feast to all ghosts released from hell as a peace offering to protect the living. The festival is rooted in the Buddhist religion, particularly regarding the story of the Urabon Sutra, in which Buddha helps a priest care for his emaciated deceased mother who manifested as a "hungry ghost." Most ghost stories are associated with tragic events or those with unfinished business.

Places that have been witness to large numbers of deaths and suffering, such as old battlefields, asylums and tuberculosis hospitals, are some of the highest-recommended places to visit if one is looking to have a paranormal experience. The *Queen Mary*, currently docked in Long Beach, California, served as both a luxury ocean liner and military ship. To this day, staff and visitors have reported upward of fifty different ghosts aboard the *Queen Mary*. However, not all ghost sightings are rooted in depressing events or take place in locations that have witnessed tragedy. Many people have had beloved family and friends pass on after living full, exciting lives, only to witness their deceased love ones come back to do a wellness check. In fact, a report compiled by Realtor.com pertaining to home hauntings found that approximately one in four Americans believe they once shared their home with a ghost. Paranormal sightings occasionally are reported in places that you would least expect to find them. Disney World in sunny Orlando,

Florida, referred to as "the happiest place on Earth," has been reportedly haunted for decades. One specific incident happened in 1970, prior to the park officially opening. The incident involved a construction worker by the name of George who died while building the Pirates of the Caribbean ride. He is speculated to have either fallen to his death or have been crushed by a giant beam. To this day, employees who are responsible for operating this ride always make sure to say "Good night, George" at the close of each shift, believing that if they do not, he will cause the ride to malfunction. Another happening, which is possibly one of the most random ghost sightings I have ever read about, was the figure spotted in the Wilmington, Massachusetts Market Basket's frozen food aisle. Christiana Bush, an employee who worked in the market's bakery, spotted an elderly lady in Victorian nightclothes and sleep bonnet standing in the middle of the aisle as though she was lost. Her face reportedly showcased a mixture of sorrow and irritability. She disappeared in a blink and could not be located anywhere in the store once she had vanished. Although Christiana received some flak for coming forward about the ghostly sighting, even by the corporation that she had worked for, she stands by her belief that what she saw was proof of the afterlife. I personally have experienced the same struggle that Christiana had when sharing my experiences with others.

For as many people as I have met who have thought my ghost stories were cool, almost as many people have thought that I was crazy for investigating the paranormal. I grew up in a normal household with a mother, father and older brother. I worked my butt off all the way through school, including at university and later a trade school, where I obtained two certificates, an associate degree and a bachelor's degree. I have worked basic nine-to-five jobs, rescued animals and purchased meals for people who have been less fortunate than I. Just like everyone else in the world, I have had my moments of sadness and depression, but I have never been diagnosed as seeing or hearing things that were not actually there. For the most part, I would like to think I have a pretty level head on my shoulders. With that being said, I have encountered so many astonishing things in my years of investigating the paranormal that I simply could not explain. I have had people around me as witnesses to some of these events, equally as amazed as I was that these happenings seemed to defy all logic.

One of my most memorable paranormal experiences before I had officially started my own paranormal team was when I took my first trip to New Orleans, Louisiana, and stayed at the Bourbon Orleans Hotel. I installed two fresh batteries in my digital point-and-shoot camera prior to taking off on a solo adventure to explore this purportedly haunted locale. As I entered the lengthy hallways, I carefully studied each area that I passed, documenting everything I was seeing via video in the event that something was to manifest. I made my way down to the second floor and admired the exquisite construction of the hotel. I came to the end of a hallway where the ballroom doors beckoned me to enter. This is not just any ordinary ballroom. It is the most historic ballroom in the entire city, dating back to the year 1817. It is known for its grandiosity and, of course, its phantom dancer. I wanted to see her in action—spinning elegantly in the air in her Cinderella-esque ball gown. As I reached for the door in eager anticipation, I heard the blood-curdling cries of a child behind me. Startled, I whipped around, letting the camera fall to my side as I tried to determine where the sound was coming from. The child's heart-wrenching sobs were so loud I found it hard to believe that other guests had not come out of their rooms or any staff had not come up to see what was going on. As I started down the hallway, the eerie cries ended abruptly. Noticing one of the hotel room doors was cracked open ever so slightly, I knocked on it at first, and no one responded. I stood back, and to my horror, the solid wood door began to open by itself, revealing a dark and empty room. Suddenly, the hysterical child began crying again—only this time, it sounded as if it was coming from every room in the hallway. I stood frozen, looking into the dark hotel room, not knowing what exactly I was expected to do. I quickly grabbed the handle of the door and closed it. As the door banged shut, the deafening sounds of crying that seemed to echo off the walls suddenly became silent. I looked around, bewildered, wondering what the hell was going on, when I heard laughter. It was not just any laughter. It was the sound of a mischievous child who was playing a prank. I ran back to the ballroom doors and crouched down in front of them, hoping to get a full view of anything happening down the hallway. The lights began to flicker, leaving me in almost complete darkness, as the distinctive laughter of a toddler echoed down the shadowy corridor. Through the darkness I could make out a tiny girl with light hair wearing a white dress. She was about four years old. Her button nose was red, and her cheeks were stained with tears. As I reached for my camera to catch her on video, she ran into the ladies' bathroom next to where I was standing. I went in after her but could find no trace of her. She was gone.

Of course, when sharing my ghost stories over the years, I have been met with skepticism, and I am okay with that. I believe it comes with the controversial role of being a paranormal researcher. Honestly, you just had to have been there. I am not out to prove the existence of anything to anyone.

In fact, I do this mainly to find out the truth of what lies beyond this life for myself and those who put their trust in me. I think being skeptical is healthy and allows for open discussion. I still cannot deny the totally extraordinary things I have witnessed, and these incredible experiences have given me hope that there is indeed more to dying than just going to sleep and never waking up again. I only wish others who are open to these types of experiences would have them as well, as I think they really challenge our beliefs of what is possible in the world.

Truthfully, the incredibly brave people who have shared their stories in this publication deserve the utmost respect. Some of these people have been traumatized by their experiences, while others have been made to feel ashamed by society. Some have been laughed at and ridiculed by former bosses, family members, co-workers and the community for sharing their personal encounters with the paranormal. It takes a lot of guts to come forward on a national scale and make yourself vulnerable to the public, just as all these individuals have done. Imagine yourself at a new job, just trying to learn the ropes and everyone's name, when suddenly you are thrust into a terrifying paranormal experience with no one to share it with. Being a victim of the paranormal can be very isolating because you desperately want answers and, at the same time, desperately want to be liked by your peers and loved ones. You don't want to come across as illogical and strange when you've never been labeled that way before. I was fortunate enough to grow up in a family that was very receptive and supportive of my ghost stories. I ask my readers, wherever in the world you may be, to keep an open mind to the stories you've read and to please respect the generous people who have opened their hearts to me for your entertainment.

I implore you to check out every location written about in this book. Gather up your friends and family and go for a ride or walk around the city. Support these amazing local businesses and seek your own truth. Maybe you will have your own spooky experiences to write home about. Most people do not appreciate their hometowns in the way that they should, and I have been guilty of that as well. When I was younger, I used to think Bay City was boring and took being born here for granted. However, when I moved away for a number of years and eventually returned home, I realized that I had missed so many things about not only Michigan but also Bay City. Once I started putting in the research for this book, it occurred to me that Bay City is anything but boring. The history of this city alone could keep one captivated for hours. Bay City was the sin city of the Great Lakes Bay region during the lumbering days. As I walk down the streets of the downtown area today,

View of commercial buildings on Water Street in Bay City, Michigan. Printed on front: "G7457 Water St. (at foot of Center Ave.), Bay City, Mich. Copyright 1905 by the Rotograph Co." Printed on back: "The Rotograph Co., N.Y., City, (Germany)." *Courtesy of Burton Historical Collection, Detroit Public Library.*

I can't help but imagine just how dangerous those streets were back in the 1800s and the many colorful characters one would have encountered on a stroll around town. Bay City sure does have a lot of reported ghost sightings in one collective area, and it is fair to speculate the reasoning behind that is due to the city's tumultuous past.

Where we go when we die continues to remain a mystery and that contributes to the fun of researching it. Some people say heaven, some say hell and some believe in reincarnation. There are people who believe that death results in coming face to face with a religious icon, and others that think death is simply a final resting place—a peaceful, painless sleep in which you do not dream and never wake. There is so much variety in stories shared around the world of people who have died that claim they know the truth about what lies beyond the grave. Many have claimed to have out-of-body experiences, claiming to have witnessed themselves lying lifeless on operation tables while doctors and nurses worked to bring them back to life. What really happens to us when we take our last breath perhaps may depend on our beliefs, our values, our character as human beings and our positive or negative mindsets. It also may be that none of that stuff will matter at all. Of course, almost everyone would prefer some version of a happily ever after, even in death. It's a no-brainer that most people would like to imagine themselves in a peaceful and comfortable paradise, surrounded by all of their favorite people, sipping on a delicious tropical drink as immortal palm trees sway softly in the wind—as opposed to being trapped on Earth in spirit form reliving their most traumatic life events repeatedly. However, only time can determine what fate we will face when our hearts expire. Life and death are both equally puzzling mysteries. No matter your views on the subject, it is always important to be kind to one another and meet others with compassion whenever possible. Life is just too short to be any other way. We're no doubt all in this crazy, unpredictable journey together, and much like Dr. Facilier's song in the 2009 Disney animation *Princess and the Frog*, if life after death truly does exist, I don't know about you, but I certainly am going to need my "friends on the other side."

BIBLIOGRAPHY

Absinthe Original. "Absinthe Drink—Absinthe Liquor with Wormwood, How 2 Drink." www.originalabsinthe.com/buy-real-absinthe-online.

Arndt, Leslie. "Bawdy Town Featurette." *Bay City Times*, 1975. Article in the genealogy room of the Alice and Jack Wirt Library.

Bay City Directories. Detroit: R.L. Polk, 1866–2020.

Bay City, Michigan. www.baycitymi.org.

Bay City, Michigan: The Way It Was. "James Shearer Is Dead." https://bcmitwiw2.wordpress.com.

Bay City Scottish Rite. "About the Scottish Rite." https://baycityscottishrite.org/about_sr.php.

Bay City Times. "Legacy of Architect Is Prominent Part of Bay City's History." 1997. Article in the genealogy room of the Alice and Jack Wirt Library.

Bay County Library System. "Historical Sage Library." www.baycountylibrary.org.

Bedell, Pamela. *The History of the Sage Library*. Flint, MI: University of Michigan, 1995.

Bergen, Tunis, G. *Genealogies of the State of New York: A Record of the Achievements of Her People in the Making of a Commonwealth and the Founding of a Nation*. Vol. 2. New York: Lewis Historical Publishing Company, 1915.

Burger, MacKenzie. "New York City Intrepid Museum Director Says Son Who Died on the USS *Edson* Is at Peace Knowing the Ship Found a Final Destination." Mlive.com, May 29, 2012.

Chapman University. "Paranormal America 2017—Chapman University Survey of American Fears 2017—Wilkinson College of Arts, Humanities, and Social Sciences." https://blogs.chapman.edu.

Dodson, Andrew. "Historic Bay City Building Avoids Wrecking Ball, Lands Developer." Mlive.com, June 2, 2016.

———. "Sage Library's 130th Birthday Lets Bay City Residents Take Ride Down Memory Lane." Mlive.com, January 17, 2014.

Herek, Raymond. "Catacombs Lured Shanty Boys." *Bay City Times*, 1973. Article in the genealogy room of the Alice and Jack Wirt Library.

History.com. "History of Ghost Stories." www.history.com.

Hull Number. "USS Edson (DD-946) Deployments & History." hullnumber.com.

Jenkins, John Philip. "Prostitution." *Encyclopedia Britannica*, www.britannica.com.

Korth, Robin. "Tour Hell's Half Mile with the Historical Society." Route Bay City, July 11, 2019. www.secondwavemedia.com.

Laidman, Jenny. "Traditions Live on in Historic Lodge Building." *Bay City Times*, n.d.

LaLonde, Pati. "Meet Your Neighbor: Howard Schmidt, 75, Owner of Coif Salon." Mlive.com, January 21, 2019.

———. "Memorial Presbyterian Church in Bay City Holding Final Service Jan. 11, Closing Doors After 123 Years." Mlive.com, January 20, 2019.

Live Science Staff. "Americans' Beliefs in Paranormal Phenomena (Infographic)." www.livescience.com.

Marchant, Robert. "The True Story behind the CT Doll at Center of 'Annabelle' Film Series." GtInsider, June 29, 2019. www.ctinsider.com.

Metropolitan Museum of Art. "Mourning Ensemble." www.metmuseum.org/art/collection/search/159185.

Michaelson, Rob. "Is This Market Basket Haunted? Ghost Sighting at Wilmington Market Basket Goes Viral." NBC Boston, March 26, 2019. www.nbcboston.com.

Michigan Meetings and Events. "Bay City Reimagined—Again | Michigan." https://mi.meetingsmags.com.

MMCC. "Jailed Tart, Leopard Trainer Die in Old City Hall; Gang Duo Nabbed." www.mybaycity.com.

Morden, Marjo. "The Not-So-Secret History of Bay City's Masonic Temple." Route Bay City, April 11, 2019. www.secondwavemedia.com.

National Park Service. "Bay City Masonic Temple." www.nps.gov/nr/feature/places/16000216.htm.

———. "National Register of Historic Places Registration Form." 1997.

New England Society for Psychic Research. "Occult Museum Tours." www. warrens.net.

New World Encyclopedia. "Burlesque." www.newworldencyclopedia.org/ entry/Burlesque.

"Obituary: Mr. James Goodrow, Auburn, Dec 12, 2019." www.legacy.com.

Office of Professional Licensure and Certification. "About the Board | Board of Barbering, Cosmetology, and Esthetics." www.oplc.nh.gov/ cosmetology/about.htm.

Olsen, Richard W. "Absinthe and Γ-Aminobutyric Acid Receptors." *Proceedings of the National Academy of Sciences* 97, no. 9 (2000): 4417–418.

*Portrait and Biographical Record of Saginaw and Bay Counties, Michigan: Containing Biographical Sketches of Prominent and Representative Citizens, Together with Biographies of All the Governors of the State, and of the Presidents of the United State*s. Chicago: Biographical Publishing Company, 1892. https://quod. lib.umich.edu/m/micounty/3930365.0001.001?view=toc.

Rogers, Dave. "Ghosts Boost Edson: Paranormals Return Nov. 22 Hoping to Be Spooked." My Bay City, November 14, 2014. mybaycity.com

———. "Heritage Found! Fabian Joe Fournier's Canadian Roots Revealed." My Bay City, April 6, 2017. mybaycity.com

———. "Slain Manager Is State Theatre Spectre, Has Reserved Balcony Seat." My Bay City, October 19, 2011. mybaycity.com

Roncace, Kelly. "Which Walt Disney World Ride Might Actually Be Haunted? | Paranormal Corner - NJ.Com." NJ.com, March 21, 2016.

Scribner, Herb. "Report: 1 in 4 Americans Believe They Live in a Haunted House." *Deseret News*, October 31, 2018. www.deseret.com.

Simeon, Bill. 2019. "Bay City Reimagined—Again | Michigan." Michigan Meetings and Events, https://mi.meetingsmags.com.

Sonnenberg, Mike. *Lost in Michigan: Hell's Half Mile in Bay City*. Bay City, MI: Etaoin Publishing, 2017.

Spivack, Emily. "The History of the Flapper, Part 4: Emboldened by the Bob." Smithsonian, www.smithsonianmag.com.

Stanton, Ryan. 2009. "Sage Library Workers, Patrons Celebrate Its History during 125th Anniversary." Mlive, January 5, 2009. www.mlive.com.

Thompson, Tok. "Why We Should Believe in Ghosts." BBC Future, October 30, 2018. www.bbc.com.

The United States Department of Justice Archives. "The Legacy of Gideon v. Wainwright." www.justice.gov.

"USS Edison History—Saginaw Valley Naval Ship Museum." www. ussedson.org.

Visit New Orleans. "Things to Do; New Orleans." www.neworleans.com.

Waraniak, Jeff. "Birth of a Legend." Hour Detroit, August 29, 2016. www.hourdetroit.com.

Waterman, Cole. "Altared Skin: 'Voodoo Tattoo' Opens in Former Michigan Church." Mlive.com, January 20, 2019.

White, Sue. "Enjoy Good Food—and Ghost Stories—at Old City Hall." Mlive.com, September 2, 2010.

Wolicki, Dale P. *The Historic Architecture of Bay City, Michigan.* Midland, MI: Bay County Historical Society, 1998.

Younkman, Tim. "Bay City's Masonic Temple Open for Public Tours, History Lesson Sunday May 18." Mlive.com, May 15, 2014.

About the Author

Nicole Beauchamp is a native of Bay City, Michigan, and received her bachelor's degree in applied science from Siena Heights University in Adrian, Michigan. With a lifelong passion for the paranormal and history, Nicole founded the Tri-City Ghost Hunters Society in 2009. Since forming the group, she has presented at libraries and universities across the state of Michigan with the goal of educating individuals on the paranormal and expressing the importance of preserving history through investigation. She has had the honor of co-lecturing with renowned paranormal researcher John E.L. Tenney, and her work has been featured in dozens of national and international publications. In 2015, she wrote a guest editorial for *TAPS Paramagazine* and was featured on Beyond Reality Radio, where she was recognized for her hard work and dedication to the paranormal by Jason Hawes, the star of Travel Channel's *Ghost Nation*. In February 2019, she was featured on the cover of *Paranormal Underground* magazine. In addition to the paranormal, she loves traveling and animals. She hopes to continue to tour Michigan in order to enlighten individuals on the spirit realm.

Visit us at
www.historypress.com
....